MODERN BUSINESS ADMINISTRATION

5th Edition

LECTURER'S GUIDE

Robert C Appleby

 Pitman

MODERN BUSINESS ADMINISTRATION

5th Edition

LECTURER'S GUIDE

Pitman Publishing
128 Long Acre, London WC2E 9AN

A Division of Longman Group UK Limited

First published in 1991

A CIP record for this book can be obtained from the
British Library.
ISBN 0 273 03333 6

Typeset by Medcalf Type Ltd, Bicester, Oxon
Printed and bound in Great Britain

CONTENTS

INTRODUCTION

The aims of the book *Modern Business Administration* are:

- to provide in one concise volume an introduction to the principal ideas and developments in the theory and practice of management/administration;
- to present ideas and developments so that they are relevant to a wide range of professional examinations, in particular accountancy, business studies, diploma in management studies, etc.

The book has been prepared mainly as a class textbook but the nature of the material is such that it can be used very effectively by independent students. Each chapter is self-contained but has appropriate cross-references to other chapters (cross-references to numbered figures or pages are to the main volume). The selection and ordering of topic areas can be varied to suit individual preferences or the demands of particular courses of study.

The use of *discussion questions* can help students and lecturers to clarify issues and chart their progress and understanding. Contemporary examples from the reader's own observations and experiences should help to increase interest in the subject and illustrate practical applications to real-life situations.

The use of actual *examination questions* from a wide range of professional bodies gives students the opportunity to gain experience in the techniques of planning and preparing their answers. The questions are not restricted to professional examinations but include first-year degree and BTEC Higher National Diploma questions.

Within each chapter of the *Lecturer's Guide* you will find:

- objectives;
- a brief summary of key aspects;
- assignments and their suggested guidelines;
- two questions selected from the review problems at the end of each chapter, with guidelines to answers except in Chapter 2 (to ease identification, the 'book' number of each question, where it differs, is given in bold print, e.g. **book question 4**);
- two additional ('supplementary') questions, with answers.

1 NATURE OF MANAGEMENT

Main objectives of the chapter
(1) Describe the concept of management and why it is needed to reach organizational objectives.
(2) List and describe the basic elements of management.
(3) Understand the complex nature of the managerial task.
(4) Identify major schools of management thought and how they evolved.
(5) Describe two modern approaches to management that attempt to integrate the various schools.
(6) State what conclusions can be reached from studies of what managers actually do.

Schools of management thought are considered – classical, behavioural, administrative, quantitative and scientific, systems and contingency theories. They all offer different perspectives on the management of an organization.

In each school there are variations in emphasis, e.g. between Taylor and Fayol. Some writers do not fit easily into a category. Most of the people connected with the *classical* school were practising managers, e.g. Taylor and Urwick. They responded to the problems of large complex organizations; hence their emphasis was on order and rationality and was largely impersonal, with efficiency and effectiveness predominant.

The *human relations* school was mainly made up of academics applying theories of social psychology to the practical problems of managers. They tended to concentrate on the informal organization and emphasized the social and psychological influences on human behaviour.

It is thought that the *systems and contingency approach* might lead to the integration of the previous schools of thought. This approach stresses the need to look at every circumstance or situation before deciding upon a course of action. The idea is that with a knowledge of the systems perspective, managers should more easily be able to strike a balance between the needs of various parts of an organization and the needs and goals of the organization as a whole.

The work of Katz, Mintzberg and others in looking at what managers really do, is of value. This is called the 'managerial roles' approach (Koontz). In essence, management should arrange to co-ordinate the efforts of people in the organization through the elements of planning, organizing, directing and controlling.

MANAGEMENT PRINCIPLES

It is quite natural for practising managers to look for a set of principles to which to turn to help them reach a decision when faced with difficult and complex problems. It is also true that principles should be critically examined as they are not eternal truths. They are preferably to be considered as 'guidelines', or generalizations which may have relevance in a particular situation.

The chapter begins with definitions of terms used, and the constantly recurring topic of whether management is a science or an art, and whether or not management is a profession. The historical development of management principles is examined briefly so that the scene can be set for a more detailed examination of recent and contemporary writings on the subject.

The need to *define the terms* used in management is obvious. Fortunately, most of the words can be fairly precisely defined. There are only a few used by the author which differ, one being the term 'element', used to describe the set of activities performed by all managers. Many authors refer to such elements as 'functions' e.g. planning, organizing, directing and controlling. Even this breakdown varies widely, but all are agreed that collectively these elements (or functions) make up a set of interdependent activities that are termed the 'management process'.

Successful enterprises must accomplish their objectives efficiently and enterprises fail most often because of poor management. The demand in recent years for professionally trained managers has greatly increased. The twentieth century has seen a great change from the 'owner–manager' to the modern 'professional manager'. Drucker considers that the emergence of professional management may well be 'the pivotal event of our time'.

Examiners still ask candidates to show their understanding of early writers, particularly modern industrial management theory which dates from the introduction of the factory system. Whatever the various ways of showing the breakdown into 'schools of thought', the following points are important to keep in mind:

- Management is an *interdisciplinary study* and its principles are derived from many fields, e.g. psychology, sociology, economics.
- Management theory must reflect the contemporary world, embrace its values and change as the environment changes.
- Each school of management thought can contribute to the existing body of management principles.
- Finally, in this short overview it must be emphasized that management is about people. Managers must work with and through people.

Therefore, the management of human resources has a significant place in the theory and practice of management.

The *managerial roles approach* was made popular by Henry Mintzberg of McGill University, Canada (*The Nature of Managerial Work*, New York, Harper and Row, 1973). He observed what managers actually do and thereby drew conclusions about the real activities (or roles) in which managers are involved. Examination candidates should be aware of the criticisms of this approach; these may be sufficiently strong to create doubt as to whether the approach is in fact adequate to found a practical theory of management.

Chapter 1 provides an introduction to the nature of the management process, which combines scarce resources to achieve organizational goals.

MANAGEMENT APPROACHES

In the 1970s and 1980s various approaches to management evolved to give us the systems and the contingency approach. Both these approaches are considered to give us integrated perspectives which can add to the established schools of management thought.

The *systems approach* views enterprises as obtaining and transforming inputs into outputs that are subsequently transferred into their surrounding environment in the form of goods and services. The outputs must be capable of being exchanged for the resources necessary to obtain new inputs. This cycle must be continually repeated for the enterprise to survive. The systems approach is useful for looking at relationships between independent parts to see how those relationships affect the performance of the overall system. It does not provide a means for solving all problems.

The *contingency approach* tries to understand the effectiveness of different managerial techniques when conditions vary, and recognizes that success in management is contingent upon circumstances that are unique in a given situation.

It is worth referring here to older theorists for a recurring theme. For example, Taylor, Fayol and Mary Follett referred respectively to:

- the need to 'choose the management best suited to the particular case';
- the fact that 'allowance must be made for changing circumstances';
- 'different situations requiring different forms of knowledge'.

Mary Follett's *Law of the Situation* mentioned the need to act in accordance with the unique requirements inherent in any situation.

ASSIGNMENTS: Nature of management

Assignment 1 Interview local business managers – two from local government and two from the private sector – and find out how they obtained their management skills. Find out which books or events significantly increased their appreciation of management and helped them to become better at their jobs. A questionnaire may be devised to bring out significant aspects. What criteria of efficiency/effectiveness do they adopt?

Notes on assignment 1
There is strong evidence that managers do not find it easy to state how they

obtained their management skills. In order to avoid 'superficial' answers a questionnaire or checklist would be helpful to bring out significant aspects. It is necessary to select carefully the managers to be interviewed and afford them time to organize their ideas enables a more considered answer to be made.

The answers to the questions are usually quite revealing and should stimulate group discussion on a number of topic areas.

One measure of success is the creation of a surplus through productive operations, and this can be expressed by an output/input ratio in a given period:.

$$\text{Productivity} = \frac{\text{Outputs}}{\text{Inputs}}$$

This is also the way *efficiency* is measured and is the achievement of ends with the least amount of resources.

Effectiveness is the achievement of objectives. It contains the idea of efficiency, but includes the wider concept of the value of the output to the overall or higher good. Drucker illustrates the difference succinctly: 'Efficiency is doing the thing right, effectiveness is doing the right thing'.

There is the problem in business of multiple objectives (see Chapter 3): individuals in an organization may have objectives of their own that differ from those of the organization.

Assignment 2   Members of the class should analyse the elements of their job and the frequency with which they occur. A *diary* should be kept for five days, using a simple diary sheet (devised by the group beforehand). Events should be filled in as they take place. *Changes in activity* would require a new line to be used.

Notes on assignment 2

The *aim* is to *analyse* the time spent on the work into categories, e.g. technical, administrative, managerial, social, personal, other. (These terms must first be defined.) Analyse the amount of time spent with other people, broken down into superiors, subordinates, people inside and outside the organization. The class should identify the percentage of activities *started* by their boss, themselves, people inside or outside the organization.

Individuals can then indicate if they are satisfied with the resulting distribution and determine whether they can (or wish to) change the results.

The research evidence (Mintzberg 1973) suggests that managers spend at least half their time in conversation with others, 40 per cent of their time with subordinates and 10 per cent with superiors.

Is it true, therefore, that the activities of most managers are characterized by brevity, variety and fragmentation?

REVIEW QUESTIONS: Nature of management

Question 1 It has been said that an effective manager is one who can change roles appropriately. What are the roles of a manager today?

Comment on question 1

The answer should discuss the managerial roles approach of Henry Mintzberg. His analysis of roles should be noted and a comment is needed on whether this approach is really an adequate basis on which to found a practical theory of management. Criticism of the approach and the link with contingency management should also be included.

Brief answer to question 1

In his book *The Nature of Managerial Work* (1973) Mintzberg comments on Fayol's principles of management and his ideas on how managers *ought* to manage rather than with how they *actually* manage. Mintzberg based his analysis on studying a group of managers and identified ten managerial roles:

Interpersonal roles
(1) The figurehead role (performing ceremonial and social duties, representing the organization).
(2) The leadership role (in charge of a unit).
(3) The liaison role (contacts with outsiders).

Informational roles
(1) The recipient or 'monitor' role (acting as a focal point to receive information).
(2) The disseminator role (passing information to subordinates).
(3) The spokesperson role (passing information to persons outside the organization).

Decision roles
(1) Entrepreneurial role (an agent of change).
(2) The disturbance handler role (resolving conflict).
(3) The resource-allocator role (allocation of all resources).
(4) The negotiator role (dealing with others, i.e. managers, customers, suppliers).

Mintzberg emphasized that the content and importance of the roles will vary according to the individual manager, the organizational context and its environment. Managers must be able to change roles appropriately and, in a given situation, identify the approach that will serve them best and help them most to achieve organizational goals.

Earlier approaches to management analysis tended to deal in universal principles that were often not applicable in specific situations. Managers today are expected to analyse the situation, adopt the appropriate role and select the most appropriate managerial techniques.

Criticisms of Mintzberg's approach are, briefly, that the sample of executives (five) was too small to support sweeping conclusions and was not comprehensive enough in classifying management activities (e.g. staff selection and appraisal, and determining major strategies, are not mentioned). It could therefore be questioned whether the executives in his small sample were really effective managers.

Question 2 Explain the systems approach to management and the advantages of using this approach in discussing management.

Comment on question 2
The first part of the question is straightforward. The systems approach should then be related to management activities, showing how it is of value.

Brief answer to question 2
A system is an organized combination of parts that form a complex entity, with interactions and interrelationships between the parts and between the system and the environment. The ideas of general systems theory are applied in formal management theory. Key aspects of systems theory are:

- Every system has inputs which interact and produce outputs. They may be either open or closed: open systems interact with the environment; closed systems have no involvement with their environment.
- Deterministic systems are those in which behaviour can be completely determined and the end results are precisely known, unlike probabalistic systems, where behaviour can only be estimated.

Thinking about management with a knowledge of the systems approach enables a manager more easily to conceptualize interrelationships of separate or contradictory ideas underlying management problems. Experienced practising managers have to deal daily with a network of interrelated elements, which involve interaction between environments inside or outside their companies.

There are planning, organizational and control systems, and within them many subsystems, for example delegation and budgeting systems. Systems approaches encourage cutting across traditional boundaries of responsibility between departments in order to appreciate the objectives of the whole organization.

Traditional management theory and behavioural science have provided guidelines to cope with uncertainty and change. General systems theory provides valuable insights into the structure and process of management.

Other advantages of the systems approach to management include:

- it emphasizes the importance of feedback for control;
- it creates an awareness of sub-systems, each having potentially conflicting goals which need to be brought into consideration;
- acknowledging the importance of the environment of a system;
- helping to understand the need to integrate the activities of the organization in order to achieve a common objective;

- it has encouraged the development of formal systems of *planning and control* and allowed the introduction of mathematical techniques into these areas of management.

SUPPLEMENTARY QUESTIONS: Nature of management

Supplementary question 1 Compare and contrast the main features of the work of the classical school of management and the human relations school, and comment critically upon the schools.

Comment on supplementary question 1

Knowledge of the two models of management is needed and they should be compared and contrasted. Criticisms of both schools should then be made. Methods of investigation used should be noted as they indicate differences in approach. Similarities or overlap of ideas should also be noted. The answer that follows is fuller than many of those given for other questions and is what might be expected of students in about 40 minutes.

Answer to supplementary question 1

The classical school was the first systematic approach to management thought. A main feature was the emphasis on finding ways to get the work done faster. Employees were thought to choose a course of action that maximized their personal economic gain, and this accounted for the emphasis on financial incentives. Practitioners were joined by researchers and recognized the emotional aspect of human behaviour, assuming it could be controlled by the logical structuring of jobs and schedules of work.

Writers representing the classical school were Taylor, Gantt, Gilbreth and Fayol. The classical school was concerned with maximizing the productive efficiency of workers (and their earnings) and understanding the process of management by means of the scientific study of work and the analysis of organizational design.

The human relations school which followed, was represented by Mayo and Follett and concentrated upon people and their needs, while still being concerned with efficiency. Their work included studies of morale and group co-ordination, which were considered central to productivity. They were principally concerned with using people efficiently and treating them well.

The classical school can be divided into two historical philosophies of management: the scientific management and administrative management approaches. Scientific management is associated with Taylor and emerged from his studies of job analysis, where measurement was essential to his method of investigation. He was concerned with efficiency, measured and evaluated in terms of productivity. He experimented in finding 'the best way' of doing jobs; this resulted in time standards and detailed planning with close inspection to ensure standards were maintained. Employees would be motivated by economic rewards and control was through a rigid hierarchical management structure. The administrative management philosophy was illustrated by the French writer Fayol, who searched for guidelines to operate a large complex manufacturing organization. He formulated fourteen principles which managers should use.

Criticisms of the classical school were that workers were treated as simply factors of production and the complexities of their emotional behaviour were ignored. Fayol's principles were considered too crude and general and unable to be tested effectively. However, the approach is still attractive to many managers as it is simple and clearly defined.

The human relations school stressed the importance of morale and motivation and the need to recognize effort and security. This approach can be considered a reaction to the impersonal nature of the classical approaches. Where the classical approach concentrated on the specific *job* being done by the workers, the human relations approach focused on the *workers* doing the job. The school emphasized the significance of the working group. The research of Mayo at the Hawthorne Plant of the Western Electric Company provided the foundation of the school's principles. Human reactions to a variety of circumstances were observed closely. Results indicated that the level of production may be set by social norms, that non-economic rewards and sanctions can affect workers' behaviour, that workers often react as members of a group and informal leadership can be effective in setting and enforcing work norms.

Other writers in the human relations school emphasize motivation by considering social needs and that the effects of work satisfaction, group cohesion and efficiency are interrelated. A satisfactory environment can assist in attaining organizational objectives.

Criticisms arise from the view that the Hawthorne Experiments were not scientific and the data was insufficient for the conclusions that were drawn. Too much emphasis was placed on the significance of groups. Some models seemed too complicated or abstract to apply to the actual work situation.

Fayol's approach appears to some critics to be too rigid and formal, whereas the human relations school tends to offer a more dynamic approach to problems and the structure of organizations. Both schools stress the importance of productivity and that management is responsible for the working environment, but they disagree on the means to achieve desired ends in production.

Supplementary question 2   What do you understand by the concept of business ethics? Suggest a framework for improving ethical decision-making in an organization.

Comment on supplementary question 2

This is a straightforward question on a topical subject. The second part of the question will carry more marks.

Answer to supplementary question 2

Ethics can be described as a set of moral principles that govern the actions of an individual or group. Business ethics is concerned with the right or wrong actions that arise in a work environment. Unlike the medical profession, managers are generally not trained to argue the ethics of their actions.

Surveys of the attitudes of European business students showed that a significant number of United Kingdom students believe that business has few morals. No one in the survey thought that business activities assist in supporting moral standards in society. This evidence has aroused interest in developing training in business ethics – no one wishes to spend his or her working life unable to feel proud of what he or she does. Reviews of various job factors showed that the one United Kingdom employees rated most important was to be treated fairly and with respect. Salary was rated only fourth. Companies looking to retain a strong competitive position by hiring good quality staff should consider this aspect of fairness and high ethical standards.

Business ethics is concerned with truth and justice and includes matters society expects, for example fair competition, social responsibility and acceptable corporate behaviour. Ethical standards are rarely discussed and they differ between different countries.

There are numerous factors to be considered in setting up a framework to improve ethical decision-making. It is important to draw up a code and the managing director should instigate this. The code should cover in outline:

- the *purpose* of the organization and the values it regards as essential in carrying out that purpose;
- general *principles* for operating the code, noting how this can be achieved;
- specific illustrations of principles and practice in day-to-day situations.

The code should be written by a *small* group that should include a legal adviser and representatives from various functions. Senior management must be committed to the code and every member of the organization should be encouraged to participate in developing and implementing it. Senior management must make available sufficient resources to achieve this aim.

Implementation of the code can be facilitated by a comprehensive training programme at all levels. This helps to reinforce group commitment. Managers may themselves need additional training before training their own staff. Alternatively, outside trainers may be used for all levels or to train a team of in-house trainers.

The training must form part of the *induction* process for new employees, thus building in from day one ethical standards that will be considered in every aspect of decision-making. In this way the firm can:

- assist recruitment and retention and raise employee satisfaction;
- enhance internal and external relations and improve staff performance.

2 BUSINESS AND ITS EXTERNAL ENVIRONMENT

Main objectives of the chapter
(1) Understand the role of business and the economic structure.
(2) Describe the role of the Stock Exchange and the new issue market.
(3) Describe briefly the information required before deciding whether or not to become involved in international business.
(4) Appreciate why managers should be concerned about the relationship between an enterprise and its environment.
(5) Briefly compare Japanese and Western European management practices.

This chapter seeks to emphasize the fact that all enterprises – public, private, profit or non-profit orientated – must consider elements that comprise their *environment*.

Managers must understand the relationship between an enterprise and its environment. A manager's performance often depends on his or her knowledge of the way the enterprise is influenced by or influences the environment.

The *private enterprise system* has been an effective economic system, particularly for most Western countries and Japan. Other economic systems must be considered. Particular note should be made of the changes in Eastern European countries and their movement away from socialism to a more mixed or free economy in which businesses and industries are privately and publicly owned in various combinations (e.g. in Poland and Czechoslovakia).

The topic of *social responsibility* is always a popular one for examiners. Its extension to embrace the protection of the environment and ecological issues is most important. Ecological goals are necessary, but they must be co-ordinated with other objectives of a societal and economic nature. Water and air pollution are major problems and are having a significant impact on businesses. Clearing up toxic waste dumps, for example, is very costly and not all companies are willing to pay these high costs. Recycling, the greenhouse and acid rain effects, conserving energy and resources are all to be considered in the changing environment of business.

GOING INTERNATIONAL

Decisions to *go international* are often stimulated by the desire to move ahead of competitors. Labour costs abroad may be lower, raw materials less expensive, or it may be that maximum economies of scale can be achieved. Going international can, however, present additional problems in countries with less stable political and economic climates.

The reasons the *Japanese* car industry decided to export and the methods they have used to reach their present position are well documented and worth considering closely.

The advantages of multinational operations must be weighed against the problems and risks associated with operating in a foreign environment. Developing countries have now acquired managerial skills and are aware of their natural resources; consequently, it is not now so easy to operate there. In some countries multinational corporations are not so enthusiastically welcomed and greater political skills may be needed.

Selection of managers to work abroad may not be easy. Although the basic principles of management apply in different countries, the practice of management can vary widely. Additional factors must be considered and to this extent an examination of the cultural environment is essential. Differences that must be noted include language, non-verbal communications, attitudes towards authority, different motivational factors and the varying nature of general values.

A comparison of British and Japanese management styles will provide good examples of differences. The main point in any comparison is not that one approach is better than another but that *all countries can add* to the theory and practice of management. A good summary of the different approaches by Japanese and American management is on page 632 of *Management,* by Koontz and Weihrich (9th edition, McGraw-Hill, 1988).

FINANCIAL MANAGEMENT

As a subject of study, *financial management* is concerned with achieving a stated financial objective for an enterprise by deciding:

- the total volume of assets a business must acquire and maintain;
- their composition;
- how the funds required for this purpose should be financed.

The tasks of financial management include raising capital, deciding the mixture of ordinary capital and debt, considering alternative investment opportunities, valuing a business, considering financial bases for amalgamations and take-over bids, and making recommendations for dividend policy.

Analysis of financial aspects of a business has its origin in accounting theory and practice, a knowledge of which is needed to understand the bases of financial analysis, asset valuation, income definition and measurement of cash flow.

A study of financial management also requires a basic knowledge of economic theory, both macro- and micro-economic. Knowledge of the theory of money and interest rates, theory of the firm and national income analysis is required for a greater appreciation of financial management. Financial managers also need a working knowledge of financial institutions and the legal framework of finance.

Chapter 2 attempts therefore to include most of the matters outlined above, which are all ingredients of the knowledge required to appreciate the role of business in its external environment.

ASSIGNMENTS: Business and its external environment

Assignment 1 You have just been appointed works manager to Woodcraft plc, a manufacturer of quality kitchenware. The managing director has asked you to prepare a short report on the potential for energy conservation within the company and to recommend a system. The following points should be noted:

- good communications are essential;
- an energy survey or audit is needed;
- the cost of the proposals;
- the need to create an energy awareness in the company.

Notes on assignment 1
It can be assumed that the company has no existing energy policy. It should be stressed that control of energy costs is a vital part of overall cost control. An energy plan is needed for a long-term period relating to future business objectives.
　　Other matters to stress include the following:

- Senior management must be responsible for and committed to the idea and their financial backing forthcoming.
- Success should be capable of measurement (e.g. reduction in energy cost per unit of output).
- Realistic targets should be set.
- An energy audit system is needed to provide basic data upon which decisions can be taken. This will record all types of energy consumed and the various uses of energy (e.g. heating, lighting, refrigeration, ventilation).
- Raising awareness requires good communication systems and a commitment by all employees. Regular feedback of results and regular training are essential.
- Periodic reviews of any energy policy are essential.
- Research has shown that after an energy survey a 10 per cent reduction in energy use is not uncommon.
- An energy manager may be needed. This post is preferably taken by a senior manager, as an additional responsibility. The energy manager should report to the board of directors or the chief executive.

Assignment 2 Form groups of six and assume each group is a committee of a charitable organization which has to award each year a cash payment of £10,000 to a business organization that has best satisfied its social responsibilities in the year.

You are asked to develop criteria for choosing firms for the award and research the activities of a number of chosen firms. Make a choice and be prepared to defend the selection in a class meeting.

Notes on assignment 2

The choice of organizations could be local or national. There is more scope at the national level where company activities are reasonably well documented.
Discussion questions could include:

- What appears to be the motivation behind the organization's activities?
- Does the group agree with this motivation?
- Can socially responsible actions taken by firms be categorized by type of action?
- Do organizations act in a typical way in matters that concern their product, their production processes or their personnel?

All organizations are today required by society to take a much broader look at the impact made by their decisions on communities and society in general. In America the term 'corporate citizenship' is often used to convey social responsibility. The meaning of social responsibility varies from industry to industry; as there are no agreed standards so there are many inconsistencies in practice.

Examples of government or state legislation that help to specify consumer rights should be noted. For example, in a speech in 1962 to the US Congress, President Kennedy described the rights to safety, to be heard , to be informed and to choose as included in 'consumer rights'. US consumer legislation since then has been based on these rights. The Ford Motor Company policies on consumer complaints are good examples.

REVIEW QUESTIONS: Business and its external environment

Question 1   Examine the factors that a company should consider in deciding upon the amount of debt to employ in its capital structure (**book question 2**).

Comments on question 1

The answer should indicate that a mixture of short- or long-term debt is usually required, with examples of each. The details of factors are straightforward, and comments on the effect of capital gearing are required.

Brief answer to question 1

In planning the financial structure of a business, a mixture of short- and long-term debt is usually required. For example, a bank overdraft is short-term debt and debentures are long term.

Factors to consider when planning choice of finance would include:

- *Cost of finance* Trade creditors are virtually costless. The cost of a bank overdraft is the rate of interest charged. Costs of leasing are the rent plus any hidden cost, if restrictions are placed on the use of assets.
- *Control* When new capital is issued, new shareholders will obtain a degree of control over the company if the shares carry voting rights, as ordinary shares generally do.
- *Risk* If a project is risky, equity finance may be preferable. An obligation to pay regular interest to a lender could be burdensome if the project fails.
- *Payment dates* Interest on debt must be paid on specific dates, while dividends on equity need be paid only when it is deemed possible to pay.
- *Claim on assets* Some types of financing may result in a charge being placed on assets, which may restrict their use.
- *Date of repayment* This must be arranged to achieve maximum advantage.
- *Loan or share capital* The choice to raise equity or loan capital will depend partly upon the capital structure of the company and partly upon an acceptable ratio between the sources of funds.

The ratio between loan capital and shareholders' funds is an indicator of financial risk. The ratio of debt to equity capital is called gearing. High capital gearing means a large amount of debt capital relative to equity. If gearing is too high, it means a company is borrowing too much in relation to its equity base. When profits are good, high gearing results in shareholders receiving a high return, as debt capital attracts only fixed-interest payments. When profits are low, there may be little profit left for shareholders after paying the fixed interest.

SUPPLEMENTARY QUESTIONS: Business and its external environment

Supplementary question 1   Describe the main external sources of finance available to a very small company.

Comment on supplementary question 1
This is a straightforward question. The small company will not issue shares to the public or be involved with offers for sale. This restricts options. A brief description of other routine sources is required.

Answer to supplementary question 1
(1) Clearing banks provide overdrafts or loans. An overdraft is flexible, relatively cheap and suitable for short-term borrowing. Loans are repayable at a future date and are not normally for large sums or for a long period.
(2) Finance houses lend at higher rates of interest than banks and are useful for short- or medium-term loans.
(3) Leasing companies buy plant and other fixed assets and lease them to companies at an agreed rent for periods up to ten years.
(4) Credit granted by suppliers is usually free and can be a useful temporary source

of finance. It should not be relied upon to any large extent.

(5) Friends and relatives may assist but the amount of the loan may not be very high.

Supplementary question 2 Various areas of the environment are said to influence organizations. These areas have been classified as social, political, economic and technological. You are asked to select three of these areas and state how they influence organizations.

Comment on supplementary question 2

This is a straightforward question which can be answered by listing factors under each heading.

Answer to supplementary question 2

An organization's *technological* environment may be said to include:

- the effect of technology on the organization's operations and competitive position;
- the amount of investment required to maintain its competitive position;
- the competitors' level of technology.

Economic influences may include:

- the availability of the right mix of labour skills at an acceptable price;
- the levels of productivity of the organization and its competitors;
- the organization's level of available resources in the form of fixed and current assets, in particular cash;
- availability of management and entrepreneurial skills;
- impact of taxation and grants and incentives available to the organization and its competitors (note the impact on companies of membership of international organizations);
- the possibly high cost of entering new markets;
- the general level of inflation: if high, this may have a marked impact on production costs, and higher selling prices will tend to reduce sales.

The *political* environment has a marked effect. Recent changes in political attitudes in Eastern Europe and the reduction of tension have caused marked falls in orders for defence contractors and the aerospace industry. The government can easily affect industries when its 'social conscience' determines, for example, that more investment is required in the National Health Service and in education.

Supplementary question 3 Describe and explain the main types of business enterprise. What are some of their advantages and disadvantages when examined from the viewpoint of a proprietor or manager?

Comment on supplementary question 3

This is basically a routine question in this topic area, with the difference that you are asked to comment on the advantages and disadvantages of each from the viewpoint of the owner or manager. The answer could be quite long as many aspects could be covered, e.g. liability, finance, control, size of business, objectives. Answers should generally be confined to just over 30 minutes.

Answer to supplementary question 3

The business of *a sole trader* is run by the owner, usually with some assistance from family or friends. The advantages include:

- Owner has control and can determine objectives and the amount of profit required.
- Owner can make decisions quickly to respond to changes in circumstances.

The disadvantages of a sole trader include:

- Finance will probably be restricted to the owner's capital and support from the bank by way of a loan or overdraft.
- The growth of the business is restricted to the owner's efforts and the amount of time devoted to the business.
- The business will need to give security to banks for loans, and personal guarantees may involve securing the loan against the owner's home, with all the resultant risks. Liability is unlimited.

A *partnership* exists when two or more persons carry on business together and the sharing of skills can enable the partnership to grow. The business is joint and profits are shared in an agreed ratio.

- Capital is provided by partners and other persons are employed. Examples are doctors' and solicitors' practices.
- Responsibility and control are no longer in the hands of one person and liabilities are shared.

Disadvantages include:

- Partners are personally liable for debts of the business (unless a limited partnership).
- Planning and control have to be good in order to ensure an effective organization with clearly defined responsibilities.
- Decisions may take longer as all partners have to be consulted and their agreement sought. Consensus may not always be easy.

Companies are organizations incorporated under the Companies Act. They have a legal identity which is completely separate from the persons who own it (i.e. shareholders). Advantages of a company include:

- In limited companies shareholders are liable only for their investment in share capital, so their risk is less than that of a sole trader or partnership.
- Management of a company can alter frequently without the company being much affected. Sole traders and partnerships rely on the continuing efforts of their owners.
- Shareholders can transfer shares and new finance can more easily be obtained by issuing new shares.

- Managements of companies are responsible to shareholders through the board of directors, and owners need not be employed by the business (e.g. public companies).

Disadvantages include:

- Ownership (shareholders) and management are separated and both may have different objectives.
- Accountability of the board of directors (management) is usually once a year (at the annual general meeting).
- The public can comment on the performance of the business from the publication of its accounts.

Public sector organizations may be nationalized industries or government departments. Their ownership resides with the state and they are managed by government officers who are accountable to a government department. They have the following advantages over private organizations:

- Their objectives can include public service objectives.
- Public money can finance them, thus enabling longer-term capital investment programmes to be instituted, compared with what most companies could afford.
- Essential industries or natural monopolies, e.g. gas, railways, can be kept under public control.
- Government objectives can be assisted by ensuring that state industries' activities are channelled in certain directions, e.g. using public money to support ailing industries.

Disadvantages include:

- There is no competition and there is often little encouragement to be efficient.
- Large-scale operations, centrally controlled, may lead to ineffective bureaucratic operations.

3 CORPORATE STRATEGY AND PLANNING

Main objectives of the chapter

(1) Explain the concept of management by objectives (MBO).
(2) Name the key result areas in which all enterprises should establish objectives.
(3) Describe the phases of the planning process.
(4) Identify the different types of decisions made by managers.
(5) Define corporate planning and briefly state why it differs from long-range planning.
(6) Describe methods of forecasting in a business and limitations to forecasts.
(7) Define the term 'management information system' and give examples of its practical uses.

This chapter deals with strategic management and planning, and economic forecasting and planning techniques.

In the past, managers were primarily concerned with making efficient use of the resources available to produce the goods and services for which their customers were willing to pay. This would, it was believed, ensure that their profits would be maximized. While the efficient use of resources is still an important concern for managers today, a more critical aspect of a firm's survival is its ability to adapt to its changing environment.

An effective strategy can help a firm to overcome the inefficient use of its internal resources. But if it chooses inappropriate strategies, it may not be able to survive even though its activities are efficient.

In this context the often-quoted statement from Peter Drucker is relevant: 'It is increasingly important that managers should first be concerned with being effective and then with being efficient. Effective means doing the right things, efficient means doing things right.' (*Management Tasks, Responsibilities and Practices*, London, Heinemann, 1974.)

In this chapter the importance of strategic planning is emphasized. *Strategy* refers to large-scale future plans which will allow a company to compete effectively in terms of its products and markets to achieve its objectives. *Strategic planning* is the process of formulating the strategy and seeing that it is carried out by members of the organization.

Reappraisal of the purpose of a business – its values and mission – is needed to ensure that it is appropriate in the present and future environment. The methods of assessing social policies and priorities should be carefully noted (page 91). In examining the management by objectives (MBO) concept, particular attention should be paid to the disadvantages (page 93). MBO is based upon the belief that the combined superior–subordinate participation in translating general objectives into individual objectives can have a positive effect on employee performance.

Decision-making is an important area of study. Decisions made by managers are often based upon incomplete knowledge. Traditional economic theory assumes management decisions are made under conditions of certainty, that managers seek to maximize expected benefits and that they are completely rational.

Criticisms of these principles were clearly stated by Herbert A. Simon, who distinguished between a theoretical economic man, who was described as rational and seeked to maximize benefits, and an administrative man, who did not make rational decisions but was bounded by limited mental capacity and by the emotions of other individuals and environmental factors over which he had no control. He was therefore subjected to *bounded rationality*.

This implies therefore that decisions made are never the optimum ones. Simon believed human beings created *simplified* models of the real situation so they could handle such information more easily and therefore considered only a *limited* number of alternatives. They therefore selected the first 'satisfactory' alternative, rather than look for the best choice (from a wider range of alternatives). The term 'satisficing' is used to distinguish it from maximizing behaviour.

Simon's concept of bounded rationality replaces the idea of economic man with a more realistic model of management decision-making.

CHARACTERISTICS OF STRATEGIC DECISIONS

This is an important topic that will be examined more closely. Strategic decisions:

- are more likely to be concerned with the *scope of an organization's activities* – they are concerned with the way management conceived its boundaries and what management wants the organization to do;
- usually have *major resource implications*, e.g. transferring part of operations abroad;
- usually *affect the long-term direction* of an organization;
- are usually *very complex* in nature as they involve a variety of considerations;
- require the *matching* of activities to an organization's *resource capability*, e.g. transferring business abroad requires staff expertise and other factors of resource.

It is helpful to consider objectives (page 77) as one of many influences on strategic decisions, and as a product of the value systems of groups and individuals in an organization.

ASSIGNMENTS: Corporate strategy and planning

Assignment 1 Break into groups of four or five and consider the extent of the effect upon a business's strategic planning of the changes in our value systems that have occurred in the last ten years. Examples of changes include the relations between:

- majority and minorities;
- individuals and institutions;
- economy and ecology.

Show how institutions that reflect these changed relations have altered the basic truths underlying the business system, i.e. profit, growth, technology, managerial authority, technical efficiency and company loyalty.

Notes on assignment 1

(1) *Profit* is being largely rejected as a *purpose* of a business, and the need is to balance this with ideas of 'social responsibility'. Profit may remain as a motivator and a measure, but a more socially acceptable statement of a business's mission and purpose may be needed.

(2) *Growth* in the economic sense has been modified as a predominant aim by considerations of quality and balance.

(3) *Technology* has progressed greatly but is being challenged on the grounds of the need for greater environmental control and safety. Developments in technology may be more carefully controlled in the future.

(4) *Managerial authority* is being challenged by demands for greater participation by employees in the decision-making process.

(5) *Technical efficiency* in production methods and in the structure of jobs is being balanced by other considerations, such as human factors.

(6) *Company loyalty* considerations relating to public interest and an individual's career development and mobility. Increasingly, the concept of company loyalty is being influenced by public interest considerations, for example, environmental issues and career mobility.

Assignment 2 In order to establish the extent to which a company's long- and short-term objectives are carefully considered, groups of two students should interview two local managers, one in local business, the other in a government agency. They are to ascertain from the managers:

- what their organizations' long- and short-term objectives are;
- the extent to which these are set out clearly in writing;
- the method adopted by each organization in its approach to the process of goal-setting.

Each group should draw a diagram to explain the process, and present it to the class.

Organizations interviewed could also be asked to show how they have considered some or all of the following objectives:

- the rate of profit and return on investment required (or other criteria of efficiency);
- the need to achieve a dominant position in the industry (or otherwise);
- how the organization ensures it maintains the values of the society in which it operates;
- the extent to which expansion into European activities is an objective.

Notes on assignment 2
The requirements of the assignment are comprehensive. It is often very enlightening to look carefully at the replies that are obtained. A surprising number of companies do not have clear long-term objectives.

REVIEW QUESTIONS: Corporate strategy and planning

Question 1   One of the basic principles of planning is that policies establish the framework upon which planning procedures and programmes are constructed. Discuss what is meant by policies and show how they are formulated and developed. One broad classification of policies deals with functions of the business – sales, production, finance, etc. Take any one of these functions and give the majority policy questions in this area, showing the factors to be considered in making policy decisions thereon.

Comment on question 1
A note on terminology is needed before dealing with the way in which policies are formulated. Then take a function that can be used to illustrate a wide range of policies.

Brief answer to question 1
Policies are general statements that guide thoughts in making decisions. They do not require action but are intended to guide managers in the decisions they make. Policy guidelines should allow managers to exercise their own discretion and freedom of choice, within agreed limits. Policies express the means by which the company's agreed objectives are to be achieved and usually take the form of statements telling members how they should act in specific circumstances.

Specific policies are easy for staff to refer to and absorb and lead to less misunderstandings than do implied policies. Policies are formulated at any level of management, and are usually formed by:

- the board of directors and senior management, who determine the main policies;
- being passed up the chain of command until someone takes responsibility;
- external influences – perhaps by specific government legislation, e.g. the health

and safety at work policy required of organizations.

Some examples of policy required in the marketing area are:

- What types of distribution channels should be used?
- What should be the pricing structure for the company's products?
- What should be the volume and type of advertising?
- What should be the credit policy?
- What method of subdivision of the sales territory should be adopted?
- What method should be used to remunerate the salesforce?
- What should be the content of the marketing mix?

Question 2 Describe what you understand by the phrase 'management information system'. In particular you should explain how the effective provision of information can assist management decision-making (**book question 8**).

Comment on question 2
This is a reasonably straightforward question which requires a precise definition. The various levels of management will have different needs and this can be illustrated in the answer.

Brief answer to question 2
A management information system (MIS) is a formal system which gathers data, compares and analyses it and then transfers relevant and timely information to managers at all levels, thus enabling them to make effective decisions. These decisions help to plan, direct and control the activities for which they are responsible.

An MIS may include the production of routine information, e.g. monthly reports, and indicate exceptions at critical points, giving information to enable the future to be predicted more accurately.

Electronic equipment enables large amounts of data to be processed quickly and economically.

An MIS can assist management decision-making in a number of ways:

- Quantitative and qualitative information can support *planning* at all levels in the hierarchy, whether strategic, tactical or operational.
- Routine decisions, e.g. stock reordering, can more easily be automated.
- Alternative plans and strategies can be assessed by simulation models or spreadsheet packages.
- *Co-ordination* is assisted by providing regular information to departments.
- *Control* is assisted by variance and exception reports, which enable checks on progress to be made and form a basis for assessment of performance.

The use of a computerized MIS is more widespread at *supervisory* levels, e.g. scheduling and daily planning. The roles of *middle-level* managers (e.g.

departmental heads) may change with the computerization of MISs. Information can be more easily retrieved by top management and thus enable more timely responses to changes in the environment. Computerization of MISs would appear more likely to affect jobs at lower managerial levels than at higher ones, as lower-level work tends to be more easily programmable.

SUPPLEMENTARY QUESTIONS: Corporate strategy and planning

Supplementary question 1 'Decision-making is the primary task of the manager.' Discuss.

Comment on supplementary question 1

This very general statement does not give any help in explaining what is involved, and often this type of question is not too well answered. Decision-making should be defined and the types of decision commented upon. Comment is needed on the nature of management tasks before deciding whether or not decision-making is the *primary* task of a manager.

Answer to supplementary question 1

Management is a social process entailing responsibility for the effective and economical planning and regulation of the operations of an enterprise. The primary task of a manager must be to utilize all resources to accomplish enterprise objectives.

This general statement does not really indicate what is entailed as it is not possible or beneficial to put management tasks in a specific order of priority. Henry Fayol analysed management activities into forecasting and planning, organizing, command, co-ordination and control. There are variations of these elements of management, all of which have a significant place in the tasks of a manager. Decision-making can be considered of primary importance in ensuring that the tasks of a manager are accomplished, as it sets in motion the other management activities.

By looking at the decision-making process, its importance can be seen:

- problems are defined and analysed;
- alternative solutions are found;
- the most appropriate solution is chosen;
- the solution is converted into a plan of action, which is then implemented.

Managers therefore take the important decisions, i.e. setting objectives and goals, defining the nature of the business, setting priorities and following up actions started. All these are the primary tasks of the board of directors. It should be noted that the manager is not primarily responsible for all decisions, many of which are delegated to subordinates. An analysis of the types of decisions will show this distinction.

- *Strategic* decisions relate to basic objectives and may affect productivity,

23

organization or operation of the business and are basically entrepreneurial and risk-taking. They are made by the board and illustrate the aspects referred to in the question. Many decisions are corporate and do not involve an individual manager.
- Decisions referring to the organization and control of resources, e.g. construction of budgets and the organization of duties, are the prime responsibility of a departmental manager and can be considered a prime responsibility.

(Other categories of decisions can be considered, e.g. H. A. Simon's programmed and unprogrammed decisions.)

Decision-making is a basic management skill which, together with other skills, enables managers to direct human behaviour and utilize all resources. It is important, however, to understand the various types of decisions that different levels of management can undertake.

Supplementary question 2 Why is it necessary for companies to establish and periodically review their objectives? What objectives should a business aim to achieve?

Comments on supplementary question 2
Usually some indication is given of the weighting of marks for various parts of a question. There is none in this case, but it is assumed that the second part of the question would merit higher marks. A definition of objectives is needed in the first part; examples of objectives from various functional areas of a business are needed for the second part of this basically straightforward question.

Answer to supplementary question 2
Objectives can be regarded as those ends that an enterprise would like to achieve by its operation. Objectives should be clearly stated and understood. They describe future desired results towards which present efforts should be directed.

The main reasons companies should establish and periodically review their objectives are:

- Stating objectives sets out clear guidelines as to the goals of the organization, usually in general terms. They are guidelines for action, which direct and channel the efforts of employees. They give direction to and are a source of motivation of employees.
- They provide parameters for strategic planning and the allocation of resources. They inform employees how and where to direct their efforts and can help in identifying new product opportunities.
- A review of objectives is needed to determine whether existing ones are still relevant and identify any need for new objectives to meet changing circumstances.

Objectives can be general or specific and may range in time from months to years. Strategic objectives last for a period of years in functional areas such as marketing and finance. Examples would be: to open a new spare parts section in six months' time; to diversify the product range; and/or to establish a selling agent in France during the next year.

There have been many attempts to identify those 'key result areas' in which enterprises should develop objectives. P. F. Drucker considers that objectives should be established in each area vital to an organization's existence. He named eight key areas:

(1) *Market share* – the impact of competitors and market potential, e.g. to increase market share from 15 to 25 per cent in three years.
(2) *Innovation* – e.g. to be the leading contributor to technology in the robotic industry within ten years.
(3) *Productivity* – e.g. to decrease production costs per unit of output by 5 per cent in the next year.
(4) *Physical and financial resources* – e.g. to increase the monthly cash flow by 5 per cent over the next 12 months.
(5) *Profitability* – e.g. to achieve a 20 per cent pre-tax rate of return on investment in the next two years.
(6) *Manager performance and development* – e.g. to establish two in-house training programmes for each management level during the next year.
(7) *Worker performance and attitude* – e.g. to reduce the time lost due to accidents by 75 per cent during the next year.
(8) *Social responsibility* – e.g. to increase the number of handicapped persons employed to 5 per cent of the workforce.

Sometimes objectives may conflict, but careful consideration should enable any conflicts to be resolved.

4 ORGANIZING

Main objectives of the chapter
(1) Describe the organizing process and explain why it is important to effective managing.
(2) Define the formal structure of an organization and identify the various ways an organization can be structured.
(3) Define the term 'delegation' and explain the differences between responsibility, accountability and authority.
(4) Explain the difference between decentralization and delegation, and discuss the factors that affect an organization's degree of decentralization.
(5) Describe the organizational development approach to change and the assumptions and values upon which this approach is based.

Organizing (page 115) is an element of management that is concerned with dividing work among groups and individuals and co-ordinating their activities in order to accomplish enterprise objectives.

An *organizational role* must incorporate:

- objectives which are clearly defined;
- identification of the major activities involved;
- understanding of the area of discretion of authority assigned to the activity.

The types of *departmentalization* should be clearly understood and students should be able to give examples from their own organization. Departmentalization is the grouping of jobs, resources and processes into logical areas to perform organizational tasks.

Delegation (page 138) is a most important organizing concept facing a new manager. It is the process by which a manager assigns tasks and authority to subordinates, who accept responsibility for the tasks. By delegating important tasks to employees a manager can extend his or her area of operations and it provides an excellent training for potential managers. Delegation also provides a way to break down a manager's responsibilities and assign them to subordinates who have specialized knowledge.

It is always a problem to avoid *unnecessary organizational growth*. As a firm grows larger and more complex there will be more specialists and more supervisors. Unless the organizational planner watches this carefully, there could be a reduction in output or efficiency.

C. Northcote Parkinson, a British historian, propounded a law: 'Work expands so as to fill the time available for its completion' (*Parkinson's Law*). According to Parkinson, the reasons for this were that managers wished to add to their staff to build empires and that additional paperwork was created by extra staff. Top management needs to be vigilant and very careful about making new appointments. (Students should be able to furnish examples of the operation of Parkinson's Law, from their own experience.)

Organizational conflict (page 148) should be treated seriously as an important aspect in the proper understanding of organizational behaviour. There is a need to understand the causes of conflict and to be able to control and use energies released by conflict. Students should be aware of the major sources of conflict, the benefits of conflict, and the methods of managing it.

Organizational culture (page 120) is concerned with the knowledge, beliefs and behaviour patterns that members of the organization have in common and that are learnt and transmitted over a period of time. Students may be able to give examples of slogans to indicate in a succinct way what a company stands for. For example, Sears's and Marks and Spencer's could be 'quality and price'.

The point to be stressed is that the *effectiveness* of an organization is influenced by its culture, which affects the way all the elements of planning, organizing, directing and controlling are carried out. The *values* of senior managers help to create the climate for an enterprise. Corporate leaders act as role models in setting standards.

Organizations must adapt to the specific requirements of the situation and note must be made of studies by researchers:

- *Burns and Stalker* (page 156) developed a conceptual scheme with two contrasting systems of management practices: 'Mechanistic' and 'organic'.
- *Joan Woodward's* findings (page 156) suggested that the more successful firms in her 'large batch and mass production' category appeared to be organized in a similar manner to Burns and Stalker's 'mechanistic' system. The 'small batch and unit production' and 'continuous flow production' firms were more effective with 'organic' structures. Woodward's research suggested that, to be effective, organizational design is contingent upon production technology.
- *P. R. Lawrence and Jay W. Lorsch* built upon the studies by Woodward and Burns and Stalker. They examined companies in the plastics industry and focused on the relative stability of environments. Their research suggested that more unstable environments called for more *organic* types of organization. There was a need for groupings of staff that cut right across functions so that activities could be more easily integrated.

ASSIGNMENTS: Organization

Assignment 1 Form groups of four. Assume each group is a member of Creativity Incorporated, a company which trains people to exercise their powers of entrepreneurship. To prepare for a demonstration to a group of potential clients, groups examine the contents of a daily newspaper. By using the information in the paper, each group should suggest two new firms that might be started. Report your results to the class, treating them as potential clients.

Notes on assignment 1
A 'good quality' newspaper should be used in order to obtain a greater number of ideas.

Questions arising from this assignment are:

- Is this a realistic task?
- What problems did students encounter in developing their ideas?
- Is it possible to be trained as an entrepreneur or to be more creative?

Assignment 2   Divide class into groups of four. Each group is to select a local company and interview representatives of the company's management, with the aim of finding out details of the formal organization structure. Each group should ascertain:

- why the organization was so designed;
- the types of departmentalization being used;
- whether structure causes any problems;
- how informal relationships affect the formal structure;
- whether the company is in a stable or unstable environment.

Notes on assignment 2
Accurate answers are more likely to be obtained if a senior company representative is interviewed. In the reporting back of findings, groups should be asked to include suggestions for improving the organization structure.

REVIEW QUESTIONS: Organization

Question 1   You have been selected to be the first manager of a new department which will commence operations in two months' time. The managing director has now asked you for a report indicating how you mean to set up this new department, stating especially (a) the departmental organization structure and (b) the objectives of the department.

The new department can be any *one* of the following:

- Production
- Human resources
- Accounts
- R & D
- Marketing
- Data Processing.

Comment on question 1

The answer should be set out in report form. An organization chart is needed. Assumptions need to be made of the work already done to date, as two months is not long before the operation commences.

Brief answer to question 1

(a) The human resources manager is responsible to the managing director. Other than his own staff he is staff manager with restricted line responsibility. He recommends to the managing director the human resources management policies, practices and procedures which are needed to ensure that satisfactory relationships between management and employees are maintained.

Departmental organization structure

Human Resources Manager

Employee records	Training Safety/welfare Management	Employee relations	Wages Salaries Pensions

(b) *Objectives of Department*
To be responsible for:

- Wages and salaries policy
- Training and development
- Relations with trade unions
- Organizing job descriptions and classifications
- Planning and supervising employee benefits
- Maintaining employees' life assurance plans
- Advising on human aspects of incentive plans
- Maintaining records and statistics
- Selection methods and systems of promotion.

Question 2 Evaluate the impact of the informal organization on the operation of the formal structure (preferably using illustrative examples from your own experience). Indicate whether, in your view, it is desirable for management to try to strengthen (or weaken) the informal organization, and why (**book question 3**).

Comment on question 2

The answer should define and then distinguish between formal and informal organization. The features of the two types of organization should then be noted and the effect informal organization can have on the formal structure and ways management can react to informal groupings. Positive and negative features of informal groupings should be noted.

Brief answer to question 2

Organization involves purpose, and guiding behaviour in a regular manner so that the purpose is realized. A formal organization, as exemplified by an army, is formed consciously and procedures are established to co-ordinate activities of groups in the interests of achieving objectives. Outward signs of formal organization include organization charts, control systems and a management hierarchy directing everybody's efforts.

An informal organization usually grows spontaneously and develops its own set of relationships, values and practices and exists within the formal organization from which it arose. There are no written rules or procedures, it is loosely structured and is rarely directed to achieve planned goals.

An example of such a group is when all the sales representatives in a company meet monthly to discuss sales problems and selling tactics, directly after their monthly report to the sales manager.

Any informal organization contains some structure and can have an impact on the operation of the formal structure. Management must be aware of the reasons for the existence of informal organizations, especially if they run counter to the objectives of an enterprise. They are often created as a reaction to the workings of the formal organization. Membership is derived from the formal group and seems to satisfy some needs neglected by the formal organization.

Managers have a number of options open to them in responding to the informal organization. They may ignore it, work against it, or preferably work towards absorbing it within the formal structure. By utilizing the positive features of the informal group, it is suggested that such a group can improve the level of work satisfaction of its members and lead to improved morale. Management can also use informal channels, 'the grapevine' to assist the speed and effectiveness of communication.

Negative aspects of informal groups are that they may be directly in conflict with the objectives of the company. Management could accept the positive aspects and try to see if their aims could be more closely joined to the aims of the organization. Wilfred Brown in his essay, 'Informal Organization', saw no need for an informal organization.

SUPPLEMENTARY QUESTIONS: Organization

Supplementary question 1

(a) What is the role of the 'third party' in an organizational development (OD) programme?

(b) What are the qualities, values and abilities desirable in persons acting as change agents?

Comment on supplementary question 1

A reasonably straightforward question requiring an appreciation of organizational climate and factors governing behaviour in organizations. (Most points in the answer provided should be enlarged.)

Brief answer to supplementary question 1

(a) Organizational development can be considered as an approach to the introduction of planned change. It involves a number of behavioural science techniques designed to build a more effective organization.

An agent of change or 'third party' is needed as a catalyst. The aim is to help the company solve its own problems. The third party is an intermediary between senior management, who wish for a programme of organizational development, and the rest of the organization.

The role of the outside consultant is that of a catalyst acting as a 'change agent'. This person will need to identify problems and help the organization to solve them. There will be a need to collect and analyse data and recommend solutions to help management. The third party therefore has an important negotiating role.

(b) A successful change agent will usually be professionally qualified with a background in behavioural sciences. People do not usually like change, which is a threat to routine and their role in the organization. The consultant therefore must be skilled in sensitivity training, resolution of conflict and group development.

Personal qualities needed to carry out the role will include good negotiating and communicating skills and a sympathetic appreciation of personal attitudes.

Supplementary question 2   How important is the manager's relationship with subordinates? To what extent is the success of the manager dependent upon the success of the subordinates?

Comment on supplementary question 2

The question is expressed in very general statements, and answers can vary greatly with different businesses. This type of question is not so popular and needs careful planning.

Brief answer to supplementary question 2

The relationship of managers with subordinates is extremely important. Active co-operation from subordinates is essential.

Where there are many subordinates, there will be reduced opportunities for face-to-face relationships with the manager. Relationships between subordinates and senior staff are therefore important. The manager's relationship to group working is therefore more important than with individuals.

The *extent* of power exerted by the manager is important. The types of power should be explored noting that too autocratic an attitude may preclude the development of effective relationships.

The nature of work: design groups working closely on projects need close, satisfactory relationships and free exchange of ideas. This may not be quite so important in repetitive jobs such as word processing and similar routine work.

Subordinates and managers may view their relationships differently. The subordinates may assume a change in methods of work reflects a personal attitude, while the manager may view it as impersonal and purely work-orientated.

5 DIRECTING

Main objectives of the chapter

(1) Explain why an understanding of leadership is important, and how a manager's underlying assumptions about human behaviour will influence his or her behaviour as a leader.

(2) Explain the importance of communication and identify barriers to communication.

(3) Explain the various ways motivation plays a role in most enterprises.

(4) Explain why co-ordination of the activities and objectives of an organization is necessary and the co-ordinating mechanisms that managers can use.

(5) Describe the contributions of the various theorists on motivation and state how their work is related to motivation in organizations.

Directing involves the responsibility of managers to:

- provide an organizational *environment* in which employees can be *motivated* to perform;
- ensure adequate *communication* to others;
- ensure they provide *leadership* to induce subordinates to work towards group goals with confidence and keenness.

THEORIES OF MOTIVATION

Theories of motivation can be classified in various ways.

Content theories of motivation include Abraham Maslow's 'Hierarchy of needs' and Frederick Hertzberg's 'Two factor theory'. Both approaches can assist managers in developing better working environments for their subordinates, by making available the specific types of rewards their employees want as compensation.

Process theories of motivation try to explain the reasons for goal-orientated behaviour. These theories are built upon the views of Victor Vroom. He sees motivation as a process that governs individual choice. He believed that, to be successful, a manager should show staff how focusing their efforts on the achievement of *organizational* goals will lead to them achieving their own *personal* goals.

Expectancy theory emphasizes that subordinates are most productive when they believe that there is a strong probability that their efforts will lead to high productivity, and that this in turn will result in desired outcomes, which will satisfy their deepest needs.

Managers should be aware that an important element in any process of motivation is their ability to offer and deliver rewards which subordinates desire. They must keep faith with those agreed commitments to ensure *equitable treatment* in performance/reward ratios. Employees are mainly concerned with the relative (not absolute) level of their rewards.

LEADERSHIP THEORIES

Leadership theories (page 170) provide ideas as to how subordinates and peers will respond to the leadership initiatives of managers. It is important to understand the sources of a manager's power and what can be further developed in order that managers continue to gain the support of their followers.

ASSIGNMENTS: Directing

Assignment 1   Each student should make a list of the ways in which his or her organization attempts to motivate its employees. The effectiveness of the methods used should then be evaluated and improvements suggested.

Notes on assignment 1
The group should consider the results and try to classify the methods used under relevant headings for discussion.

Assignment 2   Students should prepare a list of the leadership qualities they think might apply to:

- the current prime minister;
- the previous prime minister;
- the current leader of the opposition.

Notes on assignment 2
Time for research would be required and students should discuss their findings in class. One student should be elected (by the group) to present an agreed list for each of the above persons. It is interesting to see how the presenter is chosen and why.

REVIEW QUESTIONS: Directing

Question 1   Motivation of subordinates is an important part of a manager's job.

(a) What do you think motivates a person to work well?

(b) What steps can a manager take to motivate his or her subordinates?

Comment on question 1

This can be answered concisely. Motivation should be defined and also factors behind an individual's motives. Then practical steps to assist a manager can be noted. Discussion of various theories is not required – this is a practical question.

Brief answer to question 1

(a) An understanding of the motives of people in an organization is essential if a manager wishes to get the best results from them. *Motivating*, in an organizational context, is the process whereby a manager induces others to work to achieve organizational objectives as a means of satisfying their own personal desires. *Motivation* is the outcome of this process. Workers, supervisors and executives work hard, accept longer working hours and endure stress because they believe that such negative aspects of their work are acceptable in view of the rewards they obtain for themselves and others in their lives.

Motivation refers to the ways in which urges, aspirations, drives and needs of human beings direct or explain their behaviour. The process of motivation involves choosing between various forms of action.

Some people are motivated by money, particularly to fulfil specific economic needs. Money is an incentive up to a certain point and may not satisfy higher-level needs. Social contacts and relationships at work are another motivating factor: building effective working groups can therefore be a strong motivator. An individual's reputation or standing at work can be a strong motivator. To have opportunities to achieve and receive recognition for work done is important.

(b) A manager can take the following steps to motivate subordinates:

- ensure pay and rewards of an adequate level;
- develop a team spirit so members feel they can support others and be supported by them;
- train employees to progress to other jobs;
- ensure employees can measure their own progress and that their work and achievements are acknowledged;
- try to make the work of employees challenging and satisfying and keep them informed of matters that concern them.

Question 2 Set out in detail the role of the chairman of the board of directors (**book question 8**).

Comment on question 2

This is a straightforward question. A brief description of the nature of the board of directors will provide the background for details of the role of the chairman of the board.

Brief answer to question 2

Directors are appointed by the shareholders of a company. The board of directors is the representative of the ordinary shareholders, and may consist of executive or non-executive directors. Its work could include:

- approving the objectives and targets of executive management;
- appraising the plans and profit performance of the company;
- appraising capital expenditure policy and revenue expenditure budget;
- selecting the chief executive, or approving senior management.

In Drucker's view, the board of directors should be 'an organ of review, appraisal and appeal'.

The chairman of the board of directors is a figurehead and is often engaged in public relations activities, presenting a favourable image of the company to the general public and customers. The chairman's other functions may be said to include:

- ensuring harmony between members of the board;
- keeping in close, regular contact with all board members;
- resolving difficulties and disagreements among board members;
- presiding over meetings of the board and ensuring the functions of board are carried out.

SUPPLEMENTARY QUESTIONS: Directing

Supplementary question 1 'People only work for money.' Discuss.

Comment on supplementary question 1

The question refers to motivation at work. You are asked to discuss whether or not the statement is true.

Brief answer to supplementary question 1

People work for many reasons, not only for money. Researchers in the early twentieth century, e.g. F. W. Taylor, assumed people worked to satisfy economic needs – that monetary incentives were paramount.

The Hawthorne experiments showed that people had additional needs relating to personal relationships. Later, other needs were identified by Hertzberg and Likert, who stressed that people wished to reach their full potential (self-actualization). This implies that individuals seek more than financial returns: they wish to exercise responsibility and obtain a sense of achievement.

In summary, people work for a variety of motives based upon varied priorities. Managers must be aware of these needs and adapt to meet them.

Supplementary question 2 List the factors influencing effective teamwork. Take three of the factors and write a short paragraph on each.

Comment on supplementary question 2

This is a straightforward question which can be answered concisely.

Brief answer to supplementary question 2

The main factors influencing teamwork are leadership, size of the group, knowledge, skills and motivation of the group, group cohesiveness, norms or roles, and the nature of tasks to be performed.

(1) *Leadership*. Strong leaders can give the team:
- individual needs (practical assistance and counselling);
- team needs (development of team spirit, fair treatment);
- task needs (allocation of work, suitable and adequate resources).

The leader's style should be positive and suit the situation and he or she must be able to deal with possible group conflict.

(2) *Group cohesiveness*. This refers to the way members of a team work together and attract new members. Groups with high cohesiveness show strong loyalty to individual members and adherence to group standards and behaviours (group norms). They also have similarity of work, common social factors (e.g. social status), close proximity to one another and a smaller rather than a larger group size. There is a possible risk, though, that group needs may be put first.

(3) *Roles* are part of the way in which jobs are performed. They are affected by the expectations of job holders, their colleagues and others, concerning the way jobs should be carried out. Some roles are defined by the nature of the work by the group itself or by the rules of the organization. Roles could include the 'expert', the 'ideas person', the 'humorist', etc.

6 CONTROLLING

Main objectives of the chapter

(1) Explain the steps in the control process and why control is necessary.
(2) Summarize the issues managers have to deal with in designing a control system and the principles of effective control.
(3) Describe the budgeting process and identify the various types of budgets an organization can use.
(4) Describe various types of financial control methods and why they are used by managers.
(5) Describe the main types of auditing methods.

Controlling refers to the measurement and correction of performance so that the objectives and plans of an enterprise are accomplished efficiently and economically.

It was mentioned in Chapter 3 (page 80) that objectives should be established in areas vital to its existence. The following areas require objectives to be set: market share, innovation, productivity, physical and financial resources, profitability, manager performance and development, worker performance and attitude, social responsibility.

Objectives should be set in all areas. A good example is McDonald's, who insist on tight and rigorously enforced standards of quality.

Attention should be paid to budgetary and non-budgetary methods of control (pages 196–204).

Management control is similar to the process found in biological and physical systems. Some systems control themselves, through the feedback of information showing deviations from standards, and then initiate changes (e.g. thermostatic control).

A very important advance is the use of computers to produce *real-time systems* of control, in which information is produced while events are actually taking place. Students may volunteer examples such as airline seat reservations or electronic cash registers which immediately transmit data to a central storage facility that can be accessed at any time by management. An interesting point for discussion arises in this context. The cost of gathering real-time data can be high, but may save a few days – is it therefore worth the high cost of collection? In the control process, comparisons with standards and the analysis of causes of deviations and the development of programmes of correction all take time.

It is important to understand the concept of *human asset accounting* (page 216). Discussion can take place on whether it is necessary or cost effective to produce a balance sheet for human assets. What examples are there of companies that show such accounting information? The various advanced control techniques should be noted, particularly their limitations (page 218).

Resistance to control comes from subordinates and others in an organization. So it is important for managers to understand the reasons people resist control and how to overcome such resistance.

Points to note:

- There can be *too many* controls.
- Controls should *focus* not on activities or appearances but on *outcomes and results*.
- Controls should be *re-evaluated* periodically to see if they are still needed.
- Resistance to control may come from staff not wishing to be held accountable for results. To overcome this, programmes involving management by objectives techniques may help in changing attitudes.

ASSIGNMENTS: Controlling

Assignment 1 Divide the class into groups of four persons. Assume each group is a major shareholder in a company. Preferably using a copy of an actual annual report and accounts, each group should devise questions to ask the board of directors at next week's annual general meeting. Questions should be directed at expressing dissatisfaction with the company's financial performance as evidenced by the accounts.

The questions should be presented to the class and should cover at least the following:

- use of funds for long- and short-term investments;
- use of relevant financial ratios;
- valuation of stock;
- dividend and depreciation policy.

Notes on assignment 1
Copies of an annual report should be obtained, or relevant sections duplicated. It is worthwhile later to divide the class into two, to represent the board of directors and the shareholders. The discussion on criticisms made should be confined to financial matters as evidenced by the accounts.

Assignment 2 Your company has to move its Administration Department to a new office block 10 miles away and the move must be completed in 12 weeks, when the new computer system will be operational. Two groups should be formed to prepare a plan for the move and a critical path diagram (network) should be used to assist planning and control of the project.

Assumptions can be made and marks would be awarded for the most complete proposal, which should include a statement of the advantages of using network analysis methods.

Notes on assignment 2

It is important to choose leaders for the two groups and decide on the main factors that must be considered in the move; thereafter, assumptions can be made. Marks should be awarded for the proposal that is most complete.

The advantages of critical path diagrams include:

- they help to identify activities and events which are critical to the project;
- they provide a basis for calculating times, resources and costs involved in the project;
- they show a logical picture of the layout and sequence of events;
- they act as a focal point for actions and co-ordination and greatly assist planning and control.

REVIEW QUESTIONS: Controlling

Question 1 Discuss the practical value to organizations of human resource (or human asset) accounting as a means of measuring the value of people employed. What are the problems associated with the application of this technique, and how might they be overcome (**book question 2**)?

Comment on question 2

A definition of human asset accounting is needed and the reasons for its use. Problems and comments by researchers should be discussed and solutions can then be considered.

Brief answer to question 2

Human resource (or human asset) accounting can be defined as the process of identifying, measuring and communicating information about human resources to decision-makers. Accountancy has not valued employees as a resource. It has been suggested that failure to show a value for human assets in the balance sheet deprives shareholders and other interested parties of valuable economic information. Professor R. Likert suggested that failure to account for human resources internally encourages management to take short-run decisions at the expense of long-term economic benefit. A change of attitude should be developed to include human asset accounting as an integral part of any information system.

The uses of human resource accounting include:

- more accurate measure of return on capital employed by including human assets;
- by allocating relative human assets to different job grades, highlighting the location of organizational investments in human resources;
- valuing human assets, where such value becomes a relevant factor in mergers

and take-over decisions;
- integrating human asset values with financial accounts for reporting purposes;
- determining whether sufficient human capability is being acquired to achieve objectives.

Problems include the following:

- the period to be used to calculate the benefit to be received;
- management does not generally regard people as 'assets';
- unless the system is carefully explained to staff, and their participation encouraged, there could be an adverse reaction. Managers can overcome this problem by ensuring that communication systems are working well.

Question 2   A number of accounting ratios are used to measure the efficiency with which the resources of a company are being managed. Describe any four of these ratios and indicate how they may be applied.

Comment on question 2
A straightforward question which can be concisely answered.

Brief answer to question 2
Accounting ratios describe significant relationships which exist between various figures shown in the accounts of an organization. They enable a large amount of data to be conveniently summarized.

There are three main categories of ratios: financial or balance sheet ratios; operating ratios derived from the profit and loss account; interrelated ratios, which show relationships between financial and operating ratios.

The *return on capital employed* compares net profit with assets employed and is a reflection of the overall efficiency of the business. Care must be taken to note changes in money values over time. Capital employed should be clearly defined: usually it is the total of fixed assets and working capital. A low return may mean capital is under-employed or that capital is fully but inefficiently employed.

The *current ratio* is calculated by dividing current assets by current liabilities. This ratio shows how much working capital is available. A good guide is that the ratio should be 2:1.

An important measure of the cash elasticity of debtor balances may be obtained from the *average collection period of trade debtors*. First the average amount of credit sales per day is found by dividing total credit sales by 365. Then the average collection period is found by dividing total trade debtors (in the balance sheet) by average credit sales per day. These calculations show the number of days required to collect outstanding trade debtors – and the figure is usually too high.

The *shareholders' equity ratio* is an important indicator of financial stability. It is computed by dividing shareholders' equity (i.e. share capital plus reserves) by total assets. It is considered that the larger the proportion of shareholders' equity, the stronger is the financial position of the firm.

SUPPLEMENTARY QUESTIONS: Controlling

Supplementary question 1   What are the basic steps in the control process? Identify and explain the key considerations in each step.

Comments on supplementary question 1
This is a simple question and should be answered in a concise manner.

Brief answer to supplementary question 1
The control process consists of the following basic steps:

(1) performance standards are set;
(2) performance is measured;
(3) results are compared with standards;
(4) corrective action is instituted, when required.

When performance standards are set, they should not be too difficult to achieve. They should be clearly set out and easily measurable in as precise a manner as possible. If qualitative measures are set, end results should be clearly specified. Suitable quantitative techniques should be used in establishing standards.

It is important to ensure that performance is measured against appropriate standards and that results are fed back quickly to management. All such information should be relevant and produced on time to enable appropriate action to be taken. Budgetary systems provide important information in many control processes.

In comparing actual with standard performance, variances should be identified and made known immediately to the manager responsible. Action need be taken only when variances are significant. This process, known as 'management by exception', saves valuable time.

Finally, corrective action should be taken by the responsible managers with the minimum of delay.

Supplementary question 2   What administrative, organizational and behavioural problems of implementation may be experienced by an enterprise which is designing a new computer-based management information system?

Comments on supplementary question 2
This is a more involved question. New technology brings additional problems to any situation. The three types of problems stated assist the structure of an answer.

Answer to supplementary question 2
Any new system will have an impact upon any organization, its methods and

the people involved. Problems in designing a computer-based system are described below.

Administrative

- The objectives for the new MIS will be defined and lead to new policies and procedures. Decisions on whom is to be allowed to access the machines, the form of security, back-up procedures etc. will be needed.
- Documentation will need to be changed and all requirements for stationery etc. will need to be planned, ordered and stored securely.
- The new system will entail detailed planning and control activities, which will be more involved due to the complexity and size of the new system. Software design and the speed and volume of data being processed are some of the many problems likely to be encountered, and these activities are not easily monitored. Adequate training and preparation are essential.

Organizational

- Any new system involves changes in *structure* and patterns of work. Many systems necessitate numerous work stations using micros, with larger central units at head office, which usually retains final authority for deciding issues of decentralization. Many routine jobs would disappear and the nature of supervision could change.
- *Roles* may change. Systems analysts may affect the role of clerical staff who may need education and training to understand the changing relationships.
- Changes in structure may affect the *'political'* systems in organizations. Information would be passed quickly to a wider range of managers and this may lead to changes in the status of departmental heads.

Behavioural

- Uncertainty regarding job security and status would be prevalent, and staff could suffer feelings of inadequacy as a result of their experience apparently being considered worthless, because of the machines.
- Departments or sections may feel a loss of status, which may lead to behaviour such as interdepartmental arguments regarding access to information and a wish to retain old methods.
- Staff would expect career prospects to be generally poorer as supervisory grades may disappear and people may work in different groups or more on their own. This would tend to disrupt the existing social system in the organization. Staff may be reluctant to describe the system used or to be taught new systems. There would be a fear that the new system would find the old system to be totally inadequate, thus reflecting on their previous work.

7 MARKETING AND SALES MANAGEMENT

Main objectives of the chapter

(1) Understand how the marketing subsystem of a business contributes to the whole business.
(2) Define the process of market segmentation and its purposes.
(3) Describe briefly the importance of pricing decisions in marketing strategy and the procedures and methods adopted to meet agreed goals.
(4) Explain why an enterprise might enter the international business field.
(5) Describe briefly the minimum amount of information required by an enterprise to enable it to determine whether it should operate in another country.

Marketing must serve consumer needs and is the link between the organization and the consumer. It is a complex activity that reaches into most areas of an organization and its dealings with customers.

Marketing involves buying, selling, transporting, storing, grading, financing, risk-taking and obtaining market information. Another way of classifying marketing activities is:

- *exchange* functions – buying and selling;
- *physical distribution* functions – transporting, storing;
- *facilitating* activities – these assist the marketing manager in performing the physical distribution and exchange functions; they consist of grading, and standardizing goods;

    (i) *financing* which involves extending credit to customers and retailers;

    (ii) *risk-taking* is an element of the role of wholesalers and retailers who acquire stock for resale, according to their judgement of what customers will buy;

    (iii) *collecting market information* on goods required by customers, including customer behaviour and purchasing patterns.

Non profit-making organizations have become aware of the need to adopt the marketing concept. The increased competition from other fund-raising groups, coupled with government policies or expenditure cutbacks, has prompted non-profit-making organizations to research their market more methodically. Students can be asked to list a number of such organizations, place them into categories (e.g. public or private) and seek to identify clearly *who* are their potential supporters.

MARKETING MIX

After selecting a target market, the next step in developing a marketing strategy is to create a marketing mix (page 239) that will satisfy the needs of the target market. The elements of the marketing mix (fig. 7.1) should be clearly understood. The marketing mix is the mechanism that allows organizations to match consumer needs with product offerings.

Market segmentation (page 240) is the process of dividing the total market into several relatively homogeneous groups, and is used by both profit- and non-profit-orientated organizations.

PRODUCT LIFE-CYCLE

The concept of the product life-cycle (page 263) provides very important features for the marketing planner in trying to anticipate developments through the stages of the life-cycle. Marketing programmes will be modified at each stage, so an understanding of the characteristics of all stages is critical in forming successful strategies.

Extension of the product life-cycle is sometimes possible and it is useful to be aware of helpful strategies:

- *Adding new users.* Marketing abroad will increase the numbers of users.
- *New uses for product.*
- *Increase the frequency of use of product,* e.g. promoting watches as a fashion accessory.
- *Changing sizes of product,* e.g. smaller televisions and portable Walkman cassette players.

Developing new products is expensive and risky. Students should be able to think of examples of products not quite properly developed or tested, or poorly packaged and/or distributed. For example: why was Sir Hugh Sinclair's electric vehicle unsuccessful?

LOGISTICS AND DISTRIBUTION

Logistics is the process of strategically managing the movement and storage of materials, parts and finished inventory, from suppliers, through the firm and on to customers.

The use of systems logistics in planning and control is concerned with expanding inventory control to include other items. It implies integrating activities that traditionally have been located in different functions of business.

As long ago as 1962 Peter Drucker noted that 'physical distribution is today's frontier in business, where managerial results of great magnitude can be achieved'.

Changes in channels of distribution, the reduction in the total number of retail units and the great increase in size of large retail units, e.g.Tesco, have had a far-reaching impact on distribution systems.

Performance can be improved by using the logistics management approach to ensure that all interrelated activities in moving materials and goods from source to user are managed as a whole.

INTERNATIONAL ACTIVITIES

The easing of tension between Eastern European countries and the Western countries, the Single European Market, the Channel Tunnel and the increase in data transmission facilities give an impetus to the need for companies to consider seriously the impact of these events on their business prospects. (See 'International marketing' – page 275.)

ASSIGNMENTS: Marketing and sales management

Assignment 1   Groups of four should be formed and either the tutor or the group should select a product which is well-known in the classroom, allowing students to see and touch it.

Groups should assume they have been assigned to produce an advertising campaign for the product, concentrating upon the main issues to be included in the advertisement. The product must retain its present form and packaging.

Groups should re-form after 20 minutes and a representative should present group findings.

Notes on assignment 1
The groups should be asked to consider what were the *most important* factors that determined their decision on particular issues and why. Other factors that were considered can then be discussed.

An *extension* of the assignment can be to get groups to create a *media strategy*, so that the largest number of persons in the target market are reached. This strategy should indicate which media should be used and also the most beneficial times of the year for the promotion.

Assignment 2   Students should take a recent copy of a newspaper or colour supplement and look for examples of advertisements which:

- give a clear message in all respects;
- give a confused message or no message at all;
- seek to establish that the product should not be mistaken for a competitor's product;

- link the product to a 'green' or environmental policy.

Notes on assignment 2
The examples can be used to reinforce the object of most advertising, i.e.:

- to present information about a product;
- to arouse interest;
- to build desire;
- to put customers in a favourable frame of mind to buy the product.

REVIEW QUESTIONS: Marketing and sales management

Question 1 Comment briefly on each of the major elements normally included in the term 'marketing mix' (**book question 16**).

Comment on question 1
This is a routine type of question. A definition of marketing mix and a description of the elements with a few examples are required. There is much that *can* be included. You are asked for only a brief comment on each.

Brief answer to question 1
The marketing mix is a combination of policies and procedures adopted from time to time by a company in its marketing programme. Four groups of variables are accepted: product, price, promotion and distribution. The following shows some items under each heading.

Product	M	Price
Design	A	Basic price
Quality, variety	R	Discounts
Brand name	K	Credit terms
Packaging	E	Profit margin
	T	
Promotion		Distribution
Advertising		Channels
Personal selling		Transport
Publicity		Sales force
Sales promotion		

Product can refer to a service or physical object. The range of products offered is referred to as the product mix. The range and quality should be frequently evaluated and altered where necessary (e.g. cheap or dear cars, estate or hatchback). Branding is an important method used to sell the benefits of a product, e.g. Coca-Cola. Packaging protects the product and also reinforces the brand image.

Price is an important element of the marketing mix. In setting prices a company must consider costs of production, ability to generate revenue and profit, competitors' prices and desired market share. Price can be particularly important at certain times: for example, when costs of production are rising, where competitors change their price structure, or where new products are being introduced.

Promotion of a product includes advertising, personal selling, sales promotion and publicity. Promotional strategy seeks to bring customers, existing or potential, to a high state of awareness of a product and actively to adopt it. Customer behaviour can be identified at different stages – from complete unawareness to purchase of the product. There is a difference in the approach needed to sell to the consumer or industrial market and this will determine the amount of resources placed in areas of promotion.

Place, or distribution, is the last element of the marketing mix. This entails moving the product or service to the final consumer. This involves channels of distribution – the institutions facilitating the movement of goods and services from the point of production to their point of consumption. Customers tend to prefer shorter channels of distribution, by-passing middlemen, to gain price advantages, e.g. direct mail. Goods may move from manufacturer to customer direct, or via a wholesaler and/or retailer.

Question 2   What factors would you take into consideration when setting the price of a new product (**book question 11**)?

Comment on question 2
The key factors that need to be determined should be stated, and the answer geared to pricing a new product. Practical examples are helpful in answering the question.

Brief answer to question 2
Price is important because it is the one element of the marketing mix that produces revenue. Prices have to be geared to a number of factors, for example:

- costs of production and development;
- ability to generate adequate revenue and/or profits;
- the desired market share;
- competitors' prices.

If a company produces a new product of a type already being sold, existing prices will give guidelines. It is considered a mistake for a new company to aim to establish itself by means of selling at lower prices than its competitors, as this is no basis to gain customer loyalty. A competitive brand at a lower price may displace it sooner or later. A higher priced product should stress quality, reliability, style, etc. For a completely new product, price is often *high* initially, when the company will be almost a monopoly supplier until competitors emerge. Where a product required high research and development costs (e.g. in the pharmaceutical industry), a high price (what the 'market will bear') would be charged. Ballpoint pens and small electronic calculators are examples of consumer goods which greatly reduced in price after a few years. Sometimes a new product line is introduced and sold at a loss (loss leader) in order to draw attention to the range as a whole and to establish a share of the total market. The danger of too low a price is that the business may not generate sufficient revenue to cover operating and/or capital costs.

SUPPLEMENTARY QUESTIONS: Marketing and sales management

Supplementary question 1   What are the advantages and disadvantages of using direct selling methods in distribution?

Comment on supplementary question 1
This is a simple question which can be answered concisely. The reasons against direct selling are the reasons in favour of using middlemen. The answer is confined to a simple statement of advantages and disadvantages.

Brief answer to supplementary question 1
The advantages in direct selling are:

- to explain or demonstrate a technical product;
- intermediaries may not be fully active or sales may not be high;
- intermediaries may not be keen to accept products, especially if they are new;
- final sale price to customers may be too high, due to high profit margins of intermediaries;
- direct selling may be more economical if the market is small in volume and has a small number of customers.

Disadvantages of direct selling are:

- middlemen may have better retailing knowledge;
- middlemen can assist financially by enabling the manufacturer to recover working capital sooner;
- smaller quantities can be sold (breaking bulk) and a wider variety of products can be more easily dealt with;
- direct selling costs can be high if the market is widely spread.

Supplementary question 2   What do you understand by the term 'market segmentation'. Select two from the following:

(1) a manufacturer of machine tools,

(2) a supplier of office cleaning services,

(3) a manufacturer of PVC pipes,

and describe the likely bases on which each might segment its market.

Comment on supplementary question 2

Another fairly straightforward question, which requires a definition of market segmentation and examples under comparative headings.

Brief answer to supplementary question 2

Market segmentation refers to the subdivision of a market into groups or segments according to one or more characteristics that affect ability and willingness to buy a product. Markets are usually segregated into geographical, demographic or buyer-behaviour variables.

- *Geographical* can include climate, size of city or country, density of population.
- *Demographic* (or socio-economic) characteristics include age, sex, income, family size, social class.
- *Buyer-behaviour* includes brand loyalty, lifestyle, usage rate (e.g. heavy or light users).

(1) *Machine tool manufacturer*

Geographical
- Industrial town or cities or estates
- New towns
- European, overseas

Demographic
- Size of customer (large or small)
- Class of customer (quality or economy buyer)
- Trade group (using Standard Industrial Classification)

Buyer-behaviour
- Frequent or irregular buyer
- Small- or large-scale buyer

(2) *Supplier of office cleaning service*

Geographical
- Towns/cities or conurbations
- Local, regional or national networks

Demographic
- Size of customer (one office or many)
- Class of customer (basic or quality service)

Buyer-behaviour
- Use during weekdays only (day or evening)
- Regular or irregular users

(3) The third example (*Manufacturer of PVC pipes*) is shown below:

Geographical
- Urban/agricultural user
- Local, regional, national or international

Demographic
- Size of customer
- Type of customer (public utility, builder's merchant, construction company)
- Use of Standard Industrial Classification

Buyer-behaviour
- Regular or irregular user
- Large- or small-scale buyer.

8 PRODUCTION

Main objectives of the chapter
(1) Discuss the various roles production management may play in supporting the strategic plan of an enterprise.
(2) Explain the importance of materials management in production operations and describe newer methods used to ensure efficient use of materials.
(3) Identify situations in which repetitive production and batch production would be appropriate.
(4) Appreciate the importance of quality control and describe the new emphasis that is being used to improve product quality.

Production management (page 284) was used to refer to activities needed to manufacture products. This has been extended now to include purchasing, warehousing, transporting and other operations needed until a product is available for the buyer. The term *operations management* refers to activities needed to produce and deliver a *service* as well as delivering a *physical* product.

Products and production facilities of companies vary so much that every company will have a different system, although many problems are similar. The following factors may be relevant:

- Some products are more complex than others.
- Length of time on machine – the longer the time, the easier it is to replan.
- Amount of work which is repeatable: regular orders will have known cycle times as compared with the difficulty in controlling one-off jobs.
- Dependence on others: the more a company depends upon outside suppliers and subcontractors, the more difficult control becomes.
- Seasonal nature of work will affect workload and capacity.

Maintenance planning and control (page 311) includes all activities necessary to plan, control and record all work done in ensuring assets are kept to the acceptable standard. This includes preventive and corrective maintenance, planned overhaul, replacement, repairs and renewals, and plant modification to allow maintenance and spare parts manufacture.

A well-planned maintenance system should have:

- a complete programme for maintenance;
- a means of ensuring that the programme is completed;
- a method of checking results.

Purchasing (page 307) costs in many manufacturing organizations can account for up to 50 per cent of their sales revenue. Retailing organizations spend much more, as they sell what they buy.

Larger manufacturers, particularly those occupying monopoly positions as buyers, can exert great leverage on their supply market. Selection of suppliers is done very carefully in these organizations. Factors to be noted include long-term availability, domestic or foreign sources, technical development, single sourcing and stability of vendor.

Quality circles (page 297) comprise groups of employees from the same work area who meet regularly to try to solve quality and related problems in their sections. This concept represents a means of increasing production, raising quality levels and reducing costs through the active participation of employees.

Examples can be quoted of spectacular results. A serious problem, though, is that some managers expect results too soon from what is, after all, a voluntary, co-operative effort.

Pollution is an undesirable output of most production processes. This was referred to in Chapter 2. Pollution can affect water or air or take the form of noise. Major oil leakages, for example, are very destructive, and students will be able to give many other instances.

Anti-pollution regulations exist in most countries now. In the future, as part of their production decisions, companies will have to make a strong commitment to protection of the environment and a greater investment in pollution control.

Imperial Chemical Industries (ICI) in Great Britain has announced new environmental targets, including a 50 per cent reduction in waste over the next five years. Plants that cannot meet its new standards will face closure. It is significant that the company chairman is handling this initiative and that the objectives are over and above what is required by law and regulation in the countries where ICI operates.

The Chairman, Sir Denys Henderson, said the objectives were so demanding that some plants and processes may not be able to justify the expenditure needed to improve current standards. They would not survive, as environmental performance was not a matter of choice for chemical companies, but a precondition of remaining at the forefront of the industry.

ASSIGNMENTS: Production

Assignment 1 In groups of four, interview the manager of a factory in your locality. Find out why the company decided to locate in the area and what the benefits were from this market location. These could include transportation, labour supply and any relevant government or local authority incentives.

Each group's findings should be discussed in class and compared and contrasted.

Notes on assignment 1
The reasons for locating a company in a place are many, not always economic. It often produces interesting answers to ask if the company would locate in the same area now, if it were starting again (and the reasons why it would *not* do so).

The practical results of this assignment are that many factors are brought together in a specific context. Ideas from previous studies can therefore be consolidated.

Assignment 2 Divide the class into groups of four and ask them to examine the policies of local companies regarding quality circles (or teams). The aim is to find out how this idea is progressing. The groups should ascertain:

- the benefits and problems associated with instituting the concept;
- how each scheme operates;
- the composition of the team.

Notes on assignment 2
Other points of interest which may be asked include:

- what training was given beforehand;
- whether only rank and file workers are involved;
- to what extent ideas are accepted;
- how effective the teams are;
- whether they receive recognition for their work in the circles.

It is worth noting that the philosophy of perfect quality at source is more than just a slogan. Any system must be designed to minimize human error. Do employees have authority to slow down or stop production if quality is threatened? If employees receive quality at source training, quality circles will be more productive, allowing companies to concentrate on improving processes rather than re-working mistakes.

REVIEW QUESTIONS: Production

Question 1 What is meant by batch production? State the factors which must be taken into consideration to ensure that batches are set at an economic level (**book question 6**)?

Comments on question 1
A simple definition and a note of factors influencing the size of a batch are all that is required in this straightforward question.

Answer to question 1
Batch production is the name given to the method of production whereby a quantity of similar products is manufactured in a production run of limited

quantity. Goods produced may be for finished stock, to satisfy back orders or a specific order for a quantity of identical products. Groups of general purpose machines are needed to cope with the variety of work. Efficient planning and control are needed to cope with changes in programmes and the variety of jobs and operations. Factors influencing batch size include:

- demand;
- length of time until the next production run of the same product;
- the level of finished goods stock planned;
- economies of scale that can be achieved;
- the number of back-orders that may exist.

The optimum batch size can be determined by mathematical techniques, so that costs will be minimized and the risk of running out of stock between production runs greatly reduced.

Question 2 Why is it essential that all buying must be controlled by the purchasing officer? Give three sources of information from which the buyer can obtain details of the requirements on which to base an order (**book question 12**).

Comment on question 2
The need for centralized purchasing should be noted and three sources of information briefly described. This is another straightforward question.

Answer to question 2
The most underestimated executive is the purchasing officer, who is usually responsible for a large part of a company's expenditure. The purchasing department must secure sufficient and suitable raw materials, components and services to ensure the manufacturing process is fully supplied with all its needs. The work is highly specialized and discounts for bulk purchase can be high.

Some purchasing decisions can be risky and a small percentage saving on a large order can be worth considerably more in terms of equivalent sales value. Therefore, a purchasing officer must control buying decisions, after agreeing with financial, production and marketing colleagues. Fluctuating prices, quality and availability of materials are problems that only an experienced purchasing officer can control.

Sources of information include keeping a capability-analysis record of supplies to ensure standards are maintained. Knowledge of British Standards for materials should be obtained from the British Standards Institution. Records of past buyers' specifications will be available and may satisfy the user need. These are some of the sources of information which can assist a buyer in completing an order.

SUPPLEMENTARY QUESTIONS: Production

Supplementary question 1   Describe briefly the main activities within a production planning and control system.

Comment on supplementary question 1
This question is straightforward and a definition of terms is required first.

Brief answer to supplementary question 1
Production planning and control are central to the production process, and include planning, acquiring, scheduling and then controlling resources and other facilities needed to satisfy customers' requirements.

The production design must be translated into production instructions, then production schedules are prepared. The resources needed (labour, materials, etc.) are planned. Labour requirements will be discussed with the human resources department and materials requirements with the purchasing department. Plant capacity required will be determined and machines allocated. Production targets are set after discussions with the marketing department. As work is progressing, the control function will check that work is progressing to standard. Appropriate records will be maintained at every stage. Production output should be accounted for and all paperwork (invoices, etc.) completed.

Supplementary question 2   Write brief notes on the main systems of production.

Comment on supplementary question 2
A straightforward question that requires brief notes on the main factors of production systems.

Answer to supplementary question 2
There are three basic classifications. The methods a firm adopts for each product will be determined largely by:

- the nature of the product;
- the quantity of product to be made;
- the amount and frequency of the repetitiveness in production of the product.

Basic classifications are job, batch and flow production.

Job or unit production occurs when a customer requires a single product to be made to his specification (e.g. a ship or a suit). There is no production for stock. Production is carried out in short runs or single units and demand is difficult to forecast precisely. Network analyses and Gantt charts can help planning. It is rarely possible to obtain economies of scale.

Batch production occurs when a quantity of products or components is made at the same time. There is repetition but not continuous production. Production often is for stock or for a specific customer who orders a quantity of identical products. Batch production is widely used in industries where there is seasonal fluctuations in demand, e.g. clothing, food processing and printing.

Flow production occurs where there is continuous production of products of a more or less identical nature. Each machine is continually used for one product and special single-purpose machines are used. High output means machines should be regularly serviced. Automation – the product is automatically transferred to the next stage – plays a large part in flow production. It is used, for example, in the chemical and oil industries.

9 HUMAN RESOURCE MANAGEMENT

Main objectives of the chapter

(1) Explain how effective human resource management contributes to the accomplishment of enterprise objectives.

(2) Describe the term 'manpower planning' and list the main points to consider in instituting such a system in an enterprise.

(3) Outline the purposes that can be served by a good system of performance appraisal.

(4) Describe the sources of the various types of conflicts and methods used to manage conflict.

(5) Appreciate the importance of an effective system of management education and training and development and indicate how training can be effectively evaluated.

Human resource management (page 327) is the process of hiring, developing, motivating and appraising a suitable quantity of qualified employees to ensure activities are performed to accomplish the objectives of the organization.

Managers of *small* organizations will probably perform all these activities themselves. *Larger* organizations may use specialists called human resource or personnel managers. This position is becoming more important because of increased competition, the changing nature of the work force, involved programmes of wages and benefits and the need to examine costs more closely.

Human resources policy (page 331) must be clearly defined at board of director level and made known to everyone. The factors regarded as necessary in a human resource policy (page 332) are worth considering at length with students as they can be used to 'bring together' a range of management principles.

Manpower planning (page 332) seeks to maintain and improve an organization's ability to achieve corporate objectives by developing strategies designed to increase the present and future contribution of manpower. The stages of manpower planning are clearly stated in Fig. 9.2 (page 335). The importance of correct forecasting is vital and the various methods used should be carefully considered.

Recruiting and selecting staff is usually an expensive operation and the system should be periodically reviewed. The actual methods by which the final decision is reached should be examined carefully and relevant questions asked:

- Is the vacancy being advertised properly?
- Is the right calibre of candidates being attracted and retained?

- Are the tests and processes used giving us the right kind of information about the candidates?

The cost and effectiveness of the recruitment and selection process should be major factors for consideration by management. The annual report of companies must contain details of numbers of people employed and salaries and wages paid to them. The question can be asked: is the company getting value for money?

Training (page 344) and *development* are important areas for analysis and discussion. The changes in government approaches in these areas are numerous. The Training and Enterprise Councils (TECs) could play a significant role if they received adequate resources and they gained the confidence of the training providers and companies in their area. Copies of the TECs' Strategic Plans are available in every area from the local TEC office and are worth studying.

MANAGEMENT DEVELOPMENT

Successful companies, e.g. IBM, General Electric, ICI, are well known for developing outstanding managers. Special programmes of management development (page 346) are designed to develop leaders, not just managers. The companies:

- identify high-potential persons;
- give them practical, on-the-job experience;
- have formal plans for development and succession;
- select top positions internally.

Other points on management training methods are shown on page 351.

Blake and Mouton's managerial grid and Reddin's grid model of management behaviour both have their place in training and development programmes.

Management 'self-development' should be considered as important as programmes decided by the 'company'. There is a need to facilitate the process of a subordinate's self-development to enable him or her to become more effective. The idea is that real development takes place when managers *see for themselves* the need to change their attitudes and modify their behaviour or develop new skills.

The idea that an individual takes responsibility for his or her own learning is alien to many managers. The traditional emphasis – often on teaching rather than learning – tends to create students who are not really receptive to developing new behaviours or attitudes. There are problems, however, in individuals being responsible for their own learning:

- it demands actions and commitment;
- there may be unjustified expectations of reward;
- not all managers think they need it.

Managers need help in determining their real training and development needs. Such self-diagnosis requires information from immediate superiors, peers and subordinates, to allow managers to identify their real training and development needs.

The Management Charter Initiative (page 31) should be considered closely and the benefits and philosophy examined in detail, as it will be significant in management development from now onwards. The underlying principles should be noted. These are: that all stages of management education and development should provide open access, flexible delivery, assessment of performance and a competence-based approach; corporate and individual development plans; credit accumulation based on unit modules; and employer involvement.

ASSIGNMENTS: Human resource management

Assignment 1 From the organizations represented on the course, class members should select three safety policy documents. The class should divide into three groups and each group should evaluate and comment briefly on one document.

Notes on assignment 1
Evaluation should consider whether the four basic principles or objectives of the Health and Safety at Work Act were covered, i.e.:

- to maintain and improve the standards of health, safety and welfare of people at work;
- to protect persons other than people at work;
- to control the keeping and use of explosive or highly inflammable or otherwise dangerous substances;
- to control the emission into the atmosphere of noxious or offensive substances.

Assignment 2 Two members of the class should be selected. One is to play the part of a representative from management, the other is to act as a union organizer.

The class will act as a group of workers who will soon be voting in an election to determine whether or not a union should represent them. This election will take place shortly. The case for both sides will be presented after each of the two representatives have had time to prepare their case.

Notes on assignment 2
The two persons should prepare their case and present it to the group of workers. Each presentation should last about fifteen to twenty minutes and should seek to persuade members to join (or not to join) the union. (Note – management must not threaten workers or promise rewards for not joining the union.) Voting should then take place by secret ballot. The majority verdict will stand.

Discussion afterwards should indicate why members voted the way they did and what statements were most important in influencing decisions.

REVIEW QUESTIONS: Human resource management

Question 1   What are the essentials of a sound policy for the training of supervisors? How would a training scheme for senior management differ from that for supervisors (**book question 4**).

Comment on question 1
The first part of the question refers to a sound policy for supervisory training. This entails a method of approach which can be used generally, as there may be a problem in accurately defining the word 'supervisor'. Management is more capable of a precise definition, and a scheme can easily be presented.

Brief answer to question 1
Training for first-line supervisors is not very satisfactory in the United Kingdom. The nature of the job is a little uncertain as the power and authority of the foreman have been curtailed since the early nineteenth century. Shop stewards and middle management have taken away some of the foreman's job. A training scheme should include a knowledge of company procedures and an introduction to leadership and human relations.

Any training policy should ensure that:

- knowledge and skills required are identified;
- present levels of skill are noted;
- training needs are then identified;
- a training plan is prepared and implemented and the training evaluated.

Training for senior management is different from other categories of worker as a smaller proportion of the job content can be isolated and taught. A manager must be familiar with management techniques and know about behavioural sciences, so he can understand how employees react in certain situations. Schemes should be prepared to give confidence and judgement and to develop good timing and a sensitive awareness in handling people.

Question 2   When administered wisely, the attitude survey can be a very useful method of unearthing communication problems at all levels of an organization and of appraising the success − or otherwise − of communication methods. List the uses of a good attitude survey and state the possible disadvantages which accrue from such an operation (**book question 9**).

Comment on question 2
The attitude survey should be defined and then its uses identified. The design of a survey is not easy and there are disadvantages in its use.

61

Brief answer to question 2

An attitude survey is a systematic collection of data regarding attitudes, usually for the purpose of predicting behaviour or testing reactions, or ascertaining the relationship between attitudes and other variables. The uses of a good attitude survey are to:

- provide guidance for management regarding staff concerns;
- assist the process of communication;
- enable relevant action to be taken earlier.

Attitude surveys may suffer from the following disadvantages:

- the way the survey is designed and carried out can tend to inherent biases, for example, questions may be incorrectly phrased, leading to invalid answers;
- the methods of sampling, for example, by telephone or door-to-door, and size of sample may be too small;
- inappropriate statistical techniques may be applied giving invalid results;
- participants are often ephemeral, for example, they may be influenced by matters of current concern.

SUPPLEMENTARY QUESTIONS: Human resource management

Supplementary question 1   What factors should be taken into account when determining salary scales for managers?

Comment on supplementary question 1

The question involves many complex factors, which should be known as the topic occurs frequently in examinations.

Brief answer to supplementary question 1

The overall approach or ethos of an organization will determine its policy for salaries. Decisions on what are 'fair rates of pay' would ideally have been made, noting competitors' rates and the worth of jobs in the structure of the organization.

Rewards may be given for individual effort, and provide for career development and salary progression. Policies may include:

- *continuous review* of individuals' performance, with salary being based upon a formal scheme of staff appraisal;
- *research* being carried out into rates of pay available in the market;
- *job analysis and evaluation* to be carried out based upon a regular review of job descriptions – this would provide a sound foundation for the design of salary scales;
- *structure of salaries* should provide for career progression and allow individuals to progress in line with their abilities and aspirations.

Salary policy determination and its administration require an open and consultative climate and the involvement of relevant trade union representatives.

Suitable salary structures may be based upon age and service, with or without variations, or greater flexibility and latitude.

Job evaluation would provide data on the range of jobs, with grading systems based upon the results. The grades, degree of overlap and incremental points are determined by the groupings of jobs, and the levels of progression and performance. Some grades are based upon a hierarchical structure with defined incremental points within grades (such as most local authority schemes). Other organizations may prefer a freer movement between grades, using merit rating geared to appraisal schemes.

Once a structure is agreed it must be periodically updated as market rates and inflationary tendencies change frequently.

There is a need to note fringe benefits available and the impact of taxation rules. Strict control of budgets is needed to ensure overmanning does not occur. Salaries often form a major part of total costs in some organizations and the variety of factors outlined above should be considered.

Supplementary question 2   Organizations are increasingly using performance appraisal schemes. What do you think are the essential elements of an effective appraisal scheme? In your answer mention specifically:

- the objectives of the scheme;
- the mechanics of the scheme, including your views on who should carry out the appraisal and who should receive the information resulting from it.

Comments on supplementary question 2
This is a comprehensive question on a popular topic. The question itself provides the guide to points needed in an answer.

Brief answer to supplementary question 2
Informal appraisal of staff strengths and weaknesses takes place in most organizations; this is being complemented more and more by formal staff appraisal procedures. Appraisal is the process of reviewing and judging the worth of someone in his or her job and assessing potential for further promotion.

Schemes can motivate staff and/or provide management information. Appraisal can provide a strong stimulus as employees are aware that their efforts are being noted by managers. Others may see the potential of being rewarded for efforts, through promotion, salary increases or job satisfaction. Staff usually have little opportunity to discuss aspirations and current role with senior management.

Information gathered from such schemes is valuable for completing manpower plans, particularly in areas of staff skills shortage. It is a guide to areas of need, which can aid redundancy decisions. Apparent weaknesses will enable training programmes to be instituted. Skills which are under-utilized may be highlighted. Information received can provide a basis for salary review.

Schemes usually comprise the following steps:

(1) a report is prepared on each employee, usually yearly;
(2) the employee is interviewed;
(3) action is taken to follow up suggestions in the report and interview.

Appraisal methods may require the appraiser:

- to evaluate employees against predetermined criteria or against one another (e.g. ranking, forced distribution);
- to use behavioural techniques (e.g. forced choice) to indicate employee behaviour in special circumstances;
- to appraise against objectives (i.e. management by objectives) which were mutually set and agreed by staff and management.

The appraisal form shows a scale: the appraiser has to assess against each factor. Performance should ideally be capable of being measured objectively rather than be subject to assessment on less tangible grounds. The completed form may or may not be discussed with the member of staff. Open discussions with staff may produce platitudes rather than objective criticism on strength and weaknesses. Managers may not like open discussion.

On the other hand, motivation of staff can more easily be enhanced by open, honest communication.

Follow-up to the interview may include arrangements for training, promotion, transfer or salary increase. These are usually instigated by a person's immediate superior. Colleague appraisals or by groups of superiors may overcome criticisms of individual bias. Appraisal by subordinates or self-appraisal has limited support. A modified form of self-appraisal is becoming popular: a form of self-assessment which is then used as a basis for joint appraisal. The benefit of this method is that it is considered to be a more constructive and helpful method of improving job performance.

10 ADMINISTRATIVE MANAGEMENT

Main objectives of the chapter

(1) Understand the nature of administrative management and its role as a subsystem within the total environment of an enterprise.

(2) Appreciate that technological innovation will affect most aspects of office work and that managers should be aware of potential problems.

(3) Define the aim and scope of organization and methods in an office.

(4) Explain what is meant by electronic data interchange and discuss its potentially highly significant effect on office administrative functions.

The systems diagram at the beginning of the chapter (page 395) shows the importance of administrative services in the eyes of the author. The work of the office has continuously evolved, with the last decade bringing an accelerating change in the nature and content of 'office work'. We are now in the age of the expert system and artificial intelligence.

The trend in larger organizations is towards more centralization of information processing. Every few months bring a greater leap forward in technological developments that can aid efficiency in the office environment.

Companies in the forefront of the new technology have achieved lower costs and increased power in the market by *automating basic routine tasks* (sometimes called 'structured tasks'). Students should be able to give examples of this (e.g. a reduction in bank counter clerks).

Books referring to new roles for office workers which are worth reading are *Culture Shock – The Office Revolution* by Robert Heller (London, Hodder and Stoughton, 1990) and *The Age of Unreason* by Charles Handy (London, Hutchinson, 1989).

The impact of networked office technology on the work of an office can have marked results. The integration of electronic mail with a database record of past experience in a company and of the expertise of individuals can bring marked savings in cost and speed of action. Time is saved in meetings, for document transfer and by the ability of several persons to work in parallel.

The effect on staffing can be great. Intermediary roles such as a secretary could change greatly. A human interface between manager and keyboard may not be needed. Secretaries may need a higher level of education and training to take on a more challenging role.

Office services (page 405) are vital to the smooth running of organizations. In setting up any such service attention must be paid to the *quality* of service provided

65

as it affects all parts of the business. An efficient and reliable service can have a marked effect on profitability. The manager will have a substantial budget and be responsible for a large number of staff; any inefficiencies can greatly affect costs. Such an important role requires a suitably high place in any organization, with positive links to senior management.

ASSIGNMENTS: Administrative management

Assignment 1   Assume you have been promoted to office supervisor. Staff in your office have a wide range of ability and experience in information technology applications. You are asked to find out what the training needs are, and then devise a training programme to improve their skills. The recommendations should be in the form of a report.

Comment on assignment 1
An audit of existing skills is required. A simple form could be devised to record against headings (e.g. word processing, spreadsheets, desktop publishing) the level of skill they have reached. The future policy of the section should be assumed and action taken with this in mind to devise a training programme. Whether computer-based training or other methods are suitable should be considered in your answer.

Assignment 2   Your commercial director is attempting to make the paperwork within the organization more efficient and effective. You are asked to advise on the redesign of forms used in the organization. In a report, outline the points to which you would give particular attention.

Comments on assignment 2
Existing forms should be noted and their use confirmed. Redesign may incorporate details of more than one form. The stages of form design should include:

- list items appearing on the form and check that each serves a useful purpose;
- determine the order in which the items should appear to suit the convenience of the person *completing* the form;
- determine the order in which the items should appear to suit the convenience of the person *reading* and *using* the form;
- determine the space needed for each item;
- prepare rough layouts for a final draft.

Other points to note in form design include title, spacing, use of columns, size and type of paper used, appearance, simplicity, etc.

REVIEW QUESTIONS: Administrative management

Question 1 Discuss the stages in an O and M assignment. Explain how the investigation is carried out and the methods used for analysis and presentation of information.

Comment on question 1
The question is comprehensive and consists of three distinct parts.

Brief answer to question 1
Organization and methods is a systematic attempt to increase efficiency in an organization by improving procedures, methods and systems, communication and organization structure.

The stages are:

(1) *Briefing*. This is a discussion with those commissioning the assignment.
(2) *Preliminary survey*. Facts would be established regarding all aspects of the problem.
(3) Detailed investigation and analysis.
(4) Design of new procedures for comparative purposes.
(5) Report to management.
(6) Draft new procedure.
(7) Install and check system.

Having established the basic facts, a detailed investigation of the existing system must be carried out. Results should be expressed on charts so that all areas of enquiry are monitored. New procedures are designed in detail with the aim of simplifying operations. The old and new methods are compared using quantifiable data wherever possible. The most advantageous method is selected by management.

The selected method is installed and the new system is followed up later to check that it is functioning properly.

Methods used for analysis and presentation are procedure narrative, methods analysis, procedure analysis, string diagram and specimen chart.

Question 2 The office environment can have a crucial influence on the effectiveness of work in the office. Discuss how and why (**book question 12**).

Comment on question 2
The Health and Safety at Work, etc. Act (1974) and the Offices, Shops and Railway Premises Act (1963) have influenced environmental conditions and must be mentioned. Discussion will need to be wide ranging as many factors are involved.

Brief answer to question 2
Matters of importance to the office environment include:

- *Appearance* – a pleasant situation and well-designed building will attract staff and visitors.
- *Pollution* – any area with smoke or smells should be avoided.
- *Noise* – proximity to airports or motorways should be avoided.
- *Planning* – proposed new developments in a locality should be noted when considering the suitability of a site.

There are legal standards regarding temperature, ventilation, humidity, lighting and acoustics. These are mainly contained in the following acts:

- The Health and Safety at Work, etc. Act (1974) requires employers to ensure the health, safety and welfare at work of all employees, as far as is <u>reasonably practicable</u>. The Act also aims to encourage employers and employees to play a preventive role in promoting safety.
- The Offices, Shops and Railway Premises Act (1963) lays down requirements regarding temperature, ventilation, lighting, heating, working and space.

Ergonomic furniture, office layout, careful selection of machines and adequate working surfaces are all important in ensuring more effective work in the office.

SUPPLEMENTARY QUESTIONS: Administrative management

Supplementary question 1   What are the factors involved in computer security, and what steps would you as computer manager take to determine security policy?

Comment on supplementary question 1
This is a straightforward question. It requires some knowledge of computer operations, but mainly calls for a methodical approach to general security problems and their remedies.

Brief answer to supplementary question 1
Security of computer data can be considered by examining deliberate and accidental threats. Deliberate threats stem from direct human action; accidental threats from design maintenance or manufacturing breakdown, human errors or omissions due to carelessness, or matters such as flood, subsidence, vibrations, power failure and other electrical problems.

The main points to note include interruption of data or transmission, errors in stored data, disclosure of confidential information, removal of equipment or information, and destruction of programs.

As far as word processors are concerned, questions to consider include:

- how are tapes/floppy disks stored (safe/cabinet)?
- how is access to word processing controlled in terms of physical access and use of machine?
- does the word processor have a lockable keyboard?

- do you know exactly what type of information is stored and what is being processed?
- basic security must also include control over who uses machines and where;
- protection of machine by anchoring to desk or the use of alarms are both possible solutions.

The first step is to identify the security risks.

A *security policy* should:

- state the range of risks;
- assess the probability and consequence of each risk;
- select measures to remedy risks identified;
- agree on any contingency measures;
- arrange periodic reviews of the security system.

Recruitment of suitable staff is vital, and induction and training for contingencies are essential. (Do not overlook the fact that overtime operations may be inadequately supervised.) Procedures for authorized access must be systematically worked out, the issue of passes and security access cards or keys restricted. Unauthorized uses of keys should be monitored. Programs can be used to 'detect' and 'cure' computers infected by viruses. Auditors should be involved in designing and implementing control standards. Relevant aspects of the Data Protection Act 1984 should be incorporated in systems.

Supplementary question 2   Your organization is about to create a 'Management Services Unit'. What advice would you give the working party relating to the objectives, formation and operations of the unit?

Comment on supplementary question 2
The range of work of management services varies widely. Comments must be made on the possible divisions of the unit, the possible extent of its operations and with whom responsibilities should lie.

Brief answer to supplementary question 2
The needs of the organization should determine the size and characteristics of the unit, as the range of operations can vary widely. Management Services is a service section or department of an organization which specialises in providing support services for management. The nature of such services and the unit's poisition in the hierarchy should be made clear.

The main objectives of the department are to:

- analyse and diagnose problems;
- act as advisers when changes are being implemented;
- help management to plan to implement solutions.

Members of the department should have the skills and experience of handling management problems which 'line' managers need to have solved. The department would probably include people with expertise in management accounting, productivity services, computer systems and management techniques.

Members of the department may report to a related function, e.g. Finance. However, it may be desirable to make the department report to a senior director of the company. In turn, operational research, data processing and organizational methods departments should report to the management services manager in a large organization.

Initial projects for the unit should be selected on the basis that they have a reasonable certainty of success.

Note – the diagram on page 430 of the main book shows a comprehensive organization chart and answers could be based on this.